Contents

What Is a Christian?
BRIDGES Youth Series

Kevin Stiffler,
Youth Editor

Mary Jaracz,
Layout and Design

Published quarterly for the teaching church by Warner Press, Inc., P.O. Box 2499, Anderson, IN 46018. Printed in the United States of America. For permissions and other editorial matters, contact: Youth Curriculum Editor, PO Box 2499, Anderson, Indiana 46018-2420. Lessons based on International Sunday School lessons: the International Bible Lessons for Christian Teaching. Copyright © 1971 by Committee on Uniform Series. Scripture taken from the HOLY BIBLE, NEW INTERNATIONAL VERSION NIV®. Copyright © 1973, 1978, 1984, 2011 by Biblica, Inc.® All rights reserved worldwide.

2017 © Copyright by Warner Press, Inc.

SESSION	TITLE	PAGE

Unit I

	CHRISTIAN COMMITMENT	5
1	An Inspiring Faith	7
2	Pleasing to God	19
3	An Encouraging Faith	29
4	Faith in Action	41

Unit II

	MAKING THE DECISION	53
1	The Salvation Plan	55
2	The Eternal Plan	67
3	Chosen to Rise Above	79
4	Time to Get Busy!	91

Unit III

	THE CHRISTIAN'S FOCUS	103
1	Advancing the Gospel	105
2	Living in Humility	117
3	Looking to the Future	129
4	Praising God and Getting Along	141
5	Used to the End	153

HOW TO USE THIS BOOK	2
LEADING A TEENAGER TO CHRIST	163
EVALUATION FORM	165

How to Use This Book

The BRIDGES Youth Series is designed to help you engage students with the Word of God by meeting them where they're at and leading them *into* the Bible, *through* a time of study and engagement, and *beyond* the session to real-life application. Each session does this by following a racing theme. Just start at **WARM UP** and follow your way around the track to the **FINISH LINE**:

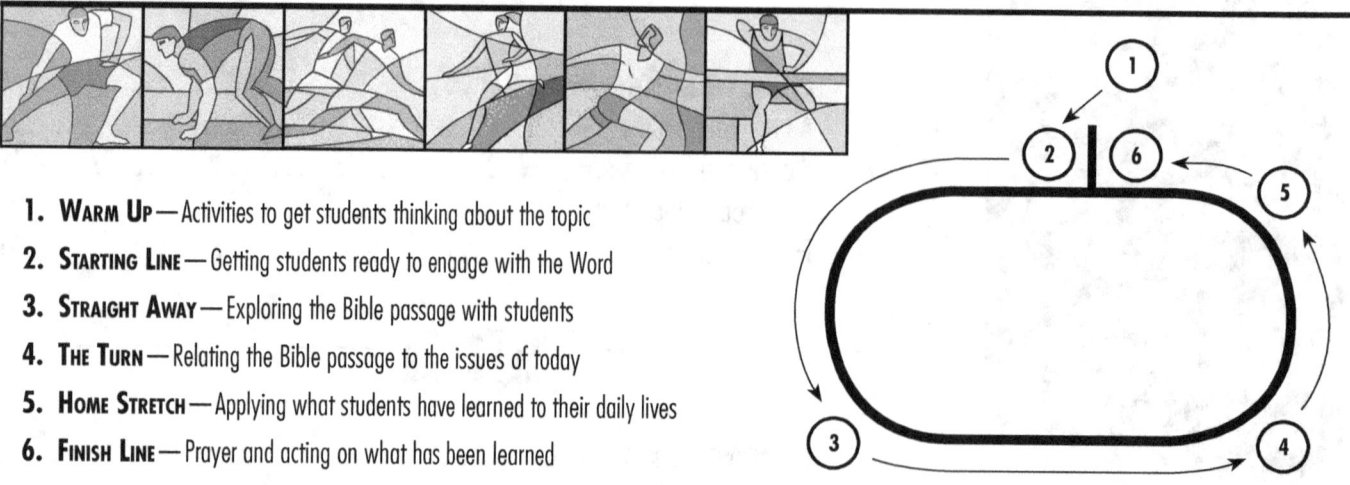

1. **WARM UP** — Activities to get students thinking about the topic
2. **STARTING LINE** — Getting students ready to engage with the Word
3. **STRAIGHT AWAY** — Exploring the Bible passage with students
4. **THE TURN** — Relating the Bible passage to the issues of today
5. **HOME STRETCH** — Applying what students have learned to their daily lives
6. **FINISH LINE** — Prayer and acting on what has been learned

The following features will help you prepare to teach and make the most of your experience:

- **Unit Special Prep** — This will let you know ahead of time if there are extra materials or arrangements needed for any of the activities in the upcoming sessions.
- **Session Overview** — This is a summary of the steps in the current session, including any resources or preparations needed.
- **Bible Passage, Key Verse, and Main Thought** — This indicates the Bible passage to be covered, identifies a key verse from the passage, and suggests the main idea that this session will communicate.
- **Bible Background** — This provides scholarly and contextual information on the Bible passage.
- **Little Prep/More Prep Options** — If you are limited in preparation time, meeting space, or classroom resources, try the Little Prep Options. If you have more time, space, and resources, try the More Prep Options.
- **Younger Youth/Older Youth Options** — If your class is composed mostly of middle schoolers, consider the Younger Youth Options. If you have a greater number of high school students, consider the Older Youth Options.
- **Reproducibles** — Each session includes two reproducible pieces that can be copied and distributed, so student books are not necessary.
- **Portable Sanctuary** — Each session has a journal-type piece to copy and send home with students. This handout will continue the ideas from the session with daily devotionals throughout the week.
- **Evaluation Form** — Your feedback is very important to us! Please take a few minutes to fill out the postage-paid evaluation form in the back of this book and send it in.

Short on time? **STRAIGHT AWAY: Explore the Bible Passage** is the core of the session. Be sure to use it, and add opening and closing elements as time allows.

Questions? Suggestions? Contact us at 1-800-741-7721 or kstiffler@warnerpress.org.

Seasons Change

I remember one afternoon sitting in my office, with the sun shining brightly in the window. However, the ground was covered with snow, and the temperature outside was about 20 degrees Fahrenheit (that's -7 degrees Celsius for you northerners!). In Indiana, the calendar can indicate that it's one season, while the weather says something totally different. Things can change drastically in a matter of hours. You definitely don't want to plant your spring flowers too soon.

I did not grow up in Indiana, but during the time I lived there, I very much enjoyed the change of seasons. There was something fascinating about watching huge snowflakes fall silently around me. As someone who gladly spends time working in the yard, I loved the fact that God used frequent rain to water the lawn there (when the lawn was not covered with snow, of course). In all seasons of the year, I find something to enjoy and appreciate. This is true no matter where I might live.

The seasons of God's nature are a perfect reminder of the seasons of life. Some are warmer than others, but God can bring good out of any of them. Perhaps in your family or job or church, you find yourself in a season where a heavy chill is in the air and nothing seems to grow. Sometimes the seasons of life move grown children out of our homes, move us on to new places of work, or move us into new places or types of ministry. Remember, life is full of seasons. Ask God to show you the beauty of the place you find yourself now. And when your seasons change, thank him for what you have enjoyed — and for all that is to come.

Glad to have a home,

Kevin Stiffler, Editor

Authors

UNIT 1

Christian Commitment

John Mize lives in Camrose, Alberta, Canada, with his wife, Twyla, and their three active and energetic boys. John loves late night shenanigans and tolerates early morning staff meetings. Coffee also rates high on his list, but not above being a husband and dad. John is a graduate of Taylor Seminary. You can sometimes find him enjoying his leisure moments on the golf course, weather permitting.

UNIT 2

Making the Decision

The different sessions of Unit 2 were originally submitted by various writers. They were compiled, tweaked, massaged, and otherwise worked on by Kevin Stiffler, editor of BRIDGES Curriculum. He enjoys playing drums, working in the yard, and spending time with his wife, Kristi, and children, Kameron and Karlisle.

UNIT 3

The Christian's Focus

Session 1 of Unit 3 was completed by Blaine Wadlow from southeastern Washington. The remaining sessions were originally submitted by various writers and were updated, modified, augmented, and otherwise edited by Kevin Stiffler, who also worked on the sessions from Unit 2.

BIBLE BACKGROUND

Bible Background was written by Merle D. Strege, former professor of historical theology at Anderson University.

UNIT ONE
INTRO
Christian Commitment

SESSION 1
An Inspiring Faith

SESSION 2
Pleasing to God

SESSION 3
An Encouraging Faith

SESSION 4
Faith in Action

CHRISTIAN COMMITMENT

In our emphasis on the free and abundant grace of God, we can sometimes lose sight of the commitment that is required of those who would follow after Christ. Jesus did not hesitate to talk about this commitment, and neither did Paul in his first letter to the church at Thessalonica.

Session 1 explores how our commitment to lead lives of faith can strengthen the faith of others. Session 2 examines how our lives should be motivated by a commitment to please God. Session 3 looks at how our commitment to giving and receiving encouragement strengthens our faith. Session 4 studies how our commitment to an active faith can bring God pleasure.

May God bless you for your commitment to love young people and disciple them in the way of Christ.

Unit 1 Special Prep

Session 1—WARM UP, Option 2 (More Prep), requires poster board, magazines, newspapers, scissors, glue, and markers. THE TURN calls for you to find a recent story of a Christian martyr. HOME STRETCH, Option 1 (Younger Youth), requires audio of the song "Wind Beneath My Wings" and the necessary equipment to play it. FINISH LINE, Option 2 (More Prep), calls for stamped envelopes.

Session 2—WARM UP, Option 2 (More Prep), calls for a copy of the Balderdash game, or a word list with definitions. STARTING LINE, Option 2 (Older Youth), requires red and green writing utensils. FINISH LINE, Option 2 (More Prep), requires the time, permission, and plans for a class service project.

Session 3—WARM UP, Option 2 (More Prep), calls for a copy of the movie *Facing the Giants* and the equipment to view it. STARTING LINE, Option 1 (Younger Youth), requires a concordance. Option 2 (Older Youth) calls for a dictionary and a thesaurus. HOME STRETCH, Option 1 (Younger Youth), requires tape and markers. FINISH LINE, Option 2 (More Prep), calls for encouragement cards and envelopes.

Session 4—WARM UP, Option 2 (More Prep), requires playing cards, and a spoon for each student. STARTING LINE, Option 1 (Younger Youth), calls for marshmallows. HOME STRETCH, Option 1 (Younger Youth), requires audio of the Newsboys' song "Shine" and the necessary equipment to listen to it. FINISH LINE, Option 2 (More Prep), calls for markers, colored paper, toothpicks, glue, playdough, cardboard, rubber bands, nails, small shapes of wood, scissors, straws, tacks, paper clips, and so forth.

Leading into the Session

Warm Up

- **Option 1** — LITTLE PREP — Imitate people, animals, and cartoons.
  Reproducible 1
- **Option 2** — MORE PREP — Create a montage.
  Poster board, magazines, newspapers, scissors, glue, markers

Starting Line

- **Option 1** — YOUNGER YOUTH — Share inspirational stories.
- **Option 2** — OLDER YOUTH — Discuss imitation.

Leading through the Session

Straight Away
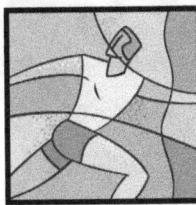
- Explore the passage.
  Bibles

The Turn
- Read about a martyr.
  Martyr story of your choosing

Leading beyond the Session

Home Stretch

- **Option 1** — YOUNGER YOUTH — Listen to "Wind Beneath My Wings."
  Audio of the song and equipment to play it; lyrics (optional)
- **Option 2** — OLDER YOUTH — Compare two evangelists.
  Chalkboard or dry erase board

Finish Line
- **Option 1** — LITTLE PREP — Complete "My Inspirational Commitments."
  Reproducible 2, pens or pencils
- **Option 2** — MORE PREP — Mail yourself a note.
  Paper, pens or pencils, stamped envelopes

SESSION 1

AN INSPIRING FAITH

Bible Passage
1 Thessalonians 1

Key Verse
You became imitators of us and of the Lord; in spite of severe suffering, you welcomed the message with the joy given by the Holy Spirit.
—1 Thessalonians 1:6

Main Thought
Our faith can influence the faith of others.

Bible Background

The books of the New Testament are not arranged in chronological sequence. Matthew was probably not the first of the Gospels, nor was it the earliest New Testament book. Among Paul's correspondence, Romans is one of his later letters. Paul's writings are ordered by length rather than date, but one of Paul's letters does claim the title of the oldest book of the New Testament. First Thessalonians was likely written in AD 49 or 50 while Paul was in Corinth on his second journey in the company of Timothy and Silas. Captivated by Paul's vision of "a man of Macedonia" (Acts 16:8–10), the little band had crossed from Asia Minor into the upper Balkans—European soil. They planted the seed of the gospel at Philippi before moving on to Thessalonica.

This city sat astride the great east-west Roman highway called the Ignatian Way. Cities along this road were important commercial centers, Thessalonica among them. From there the missionaries continued their journey, stopping at Berea, Athens, and Corinth.

Under threat of harm, Paul and his associates had been forced to leave Thessalonica hastily and perhaps prematurely. Paul was concerned for the fate of the new Christian community there, and for that reason he sent Timothy back to Thessalonica to look in on the church and strengthen it. Subsequently, Timothy returned to Corinth with his report. Timothy's positive news became the immediate cause for Paul's letter. He was delighted that the church was in good condition. He had been especially concerned for these new believers and said, "We continually remember before our God and Father your work produced by faith, your labor prompted by love, and your endurance inspired by hope in our Lord Jesus Christ" (1:3). Already in the earliest of his extant letters, Paul made reference to three central Christian virtues—faith, hope, and love. They were always intertwined in Paul's writing, but from time to time he highlighted one of them. In Galatians and Romans, Paul amplified the theme of faith. To the Corinthians, he stressed the importance of love. Faith and love were well-developed among the Thessalonians, but Paul was especially concerned that they understand and embody the virtue of hope. This hope could help pull them through times of trial and persecution. Paul trusted that it could enable them to continue to live and grow in Christ and bring to full completion the work of the Holy Spirit begun in them through Jesus Christ.

Leading into the Session

Option 1 (Little Prep)
Imitate people, animals, and cartoons.

Make a copy of "Who Am I?" (Reproducible 1) and cut along the dotted lines. Shuffle and stack the cards face-down and ask the students to take turns randomly choosing cards from the deck. The students may use actions, sounds, and famous phrases to imitate the person, animal, or cartoon character from the card. As a student does the imitation, the rest of the class must guess who or what character is being depicted. Do as many imitations as time or the number of cards allows.

Say, **Sometimes being a good imitator can be helpful to us.**

WARM UP

Note:
If you sent the Portable Sanctuary home with students last week, take some time at the beginning of this session to review and discuss their experience.

Option 2 (More Prep)
Create a montage.

Bring to class poster board, magazines, newspapers, scissors, glue, and markers. Invite the students to cut out pictures from the magazines and newspapers and to glue them to the poster board, creating a montage. The goal is to select pictures and images that represent what idols (objects of devotion, affection, or obsession) look like in our time and culture. Ask the students to use the markers to label or describe the images on the montage. When your montage is complete, take time to discuss what images your students have selected and why they selected them.

Say, **The things that are idols in our own lives speak loudly to others about what is really important to us.**

Option 1 (Younger Youth)
Share inspirational stories.

Encourage your students to share with the rest of the group stories of people who have inspired them in any particular area of their lives. You can set the tone by sharing with them a story of someone important or special in your own life who has inspired you in your faith, in your family life, or in the area of personal growth and development. After the students have had a chance to share, discuss any or all of the following questions:

- **What is it about the person you described that inspired you the most?**
- **Did this person initiate contact with you and create the opportunity for your relationship? If not, how did the relationship come about?**
- **What steps did you take to allow for or encourage this inspirational relationship to begin or grow?** Answers could include things such as these: I spent time with this person, I asked questions, I was vulnerable in sharing real struggles with this person, I allowed this person's guidance and direction to make a difference in my decision, and so forth.
- **In what ways would you like to be more like this person?**

When you are ready to move on, say, **Let's read about some people who were a tremendous inspiration to others.**

STARTING LINE

Option 2 (Older Youth)
Discuss imitation.

Utilize the following questions to discuss with your students some of the realities and pitfalls that could be at work when imitating others:

- **When is it good to imitate others? When is it bad?**
- **Is it always all right to imitate other people when they are doing good things?** That may depend on our motivation. We may imitate the good works of someone else just so we can look good or receive praise from others.
- **Would you encourage anyone to imitate you? Why or why not? In what ways?**
- **Have others imitated you when you weren't asking them to? Did you like it when they imitated you? Would you act differently in any way if you knew that someone was going to imitate your every action?** Point out that younger siblings and others often imitate us without our asking them to or even being aware of it. Like it or not, others do imitate us and look up to us.
- **Are there advantages to imitating someone who is still alive as opposed to someone who is no longer living?** Someone who is alive can clarify the reasons behind what he or she is doing and can actively influence our imitation of him or her. Someone who is not living has his or her reputation "set in stone"—that is, this person is not generating any new stories. But people can distort the truth about someone who is no longer living, and that person is not here to "set the record straight."

When you are ready to move on, say, **Let's read about some people who created a very positive example for others to imitate.**

Leading through the Session

Straight Away

Explore the Bible passage.

Read together 1 Thessalonians 1 (the whole chapter) and discuss the following questions:

- **How did Paul, Silas, and Timothy feel about the people in the church at Thessalonica?** They wished grace and peace for them, were thankful to God for them, and were constantly praying for them. They obviously cared deeply for these people. Point out that these are appropriate things for us to do as well in response for the good people that God sends into our own lives.
- **What was it that made Paul, Silas, and Timothy so thankful for these people?** The work that came from their faith, the labor that was prompted by their love, and the endurance that was inspired by their hope in Christ. These are not necessarily three different causes and effects but three ways of stating (and therefore emphasizing) the same thing: The relationship of the Thessalonians with Christ showed in the way that they lived. Point out that Paul, Silas, and Timothy had devoted their lives to sharing the good news of Christ—and it made them very happy to see that good news making a difference.

- **What indicated to Paul that the Thessalonians were chosen by God?** When Paul and the others had told the Thessalonians about Christ, it was more than just a speech or a polite conversation: there was power behind the words, the Holy Spirit moved, and the Thessalonians experienced deep conviction. In other words, God moved in their hearts.
- **What was the end result of the Thessalonians imitating Paul and the Lord?** They were filled with joy and became models for other believers throughout the region and beyond. People were amazed at how God was working in the Thessalonian church.
- **If we imitate godly men and women, what will be a likely result?** Accept any reasonable answers, but draw attention to the truth that as we imitate, others will imitate us and then be imitated by others, and so on. It's a ripple effect that touches the lives of more and more people.
- **What could have been an obstacle to the Thessalonian church in receiving and responding to the message Paul brought to them?** The text says that they experienced "severe suffering" (v 6). Point out that this was not a coincidental or unrelated distraction; they were suffering persecution because of their faith in Christ.
- **What did the people of the Thessalonian church turn away from as they turned to God? What things should we be turning away from as God calls us into relationship with him?** They turned away from idols. To them this would have been physical statues of wood or stone that people bowed down to and believed had actual powers. Encourage the students to think outside the box as they discuss some of their own struggles. There are many things in our lives that can become obsessions for us and draw our attention away from God: work, school grades, video games, popularity, brand-name clothing, music, a certain body image, sports, and so forth.
- **Do you think there is still value in writing letters to friends to inspire and encourage them in their faith? What are some other ways we can provide this type of encouragement?** Modern technology has opened up many avenues for us to encourage others, including phone calls, e-mail, Facebook, texting, Tweeting, and so forth. Point out that the message is much the same as the words Paul wrote to his friends: "I appreciate what God is doing in your life, and I'm praying for you."

Say, **Paul saw how much the faith of his Thessalonian friends was influencing the faith of others.**

The Turn

Read about a martyr.
Prior to class, take time to find a story of a recent Christian martyr to share with the class. One great resource is the Voice of the Martyrs, either their newsletters or one of their websites (www.persecution.com in the USA or www.vomcanada.com in Canada). Bring your story to class and read it to your students. If possible, find a story of someone who is of similar age to your students. After sharing the story, ask, **Why is this type of story inspirational?** Point out that persecution is not something that only happened a long time ago or while the Bible was being written. Persecution has always been a part of the experience of the Christian church, from the time of Christ right up until now. Even while your

group meets, there are those in another part of the world who are doing so in secret and at risk of their very lives.

Say, **The faith of persecuted Christians today can inspire us—and those people can also use encouragement from people such as us.**

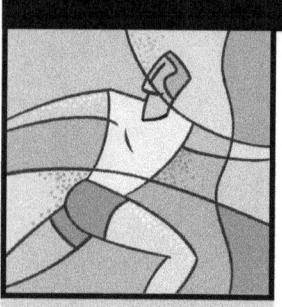

HOME STRETCH

Leading beyond the Session

Option 1 (Younger Youth)
Listen to "Wind Beneath My Wings."

Bring to class an audio version of the song "Wind Beneath My Wings" (recorded by Bette Midler on the *Beaches* soundtrack and also done by other artists). As you play the song, ask the students to listen closely to the lyrics and to think about how they apply to today's discussion. After the song is through, invite the group members to pray for the person to their right, asking that the Lord would give this person an opportunity to be this kind of an inspiration to someone that the Lord has placed in his or her life. If time allows, the students might share specifically the names of people they may be able to influence in this way.

When you are ready to move on, say, **As disciples of Christ, our witness does not depend solely on our own actions. We rely heavily on the power of the Holy Spirit to work through us.**

· ·

Option 2 (Older Youth)
Compare two evangelists.

Ask, **Does a person have to be totally outgoing and be a great public speaker in order to have an inspiring faith?** Encourage the students to consider the different personalities of two evangelists who have been very effective in sharing their faith and inspiring others.

Make two columns on the board; write *Billy Graham* at the top of one column and point out that Graham was an animated speaker who had much charisma and was very energetic in his presentation. He spoke to stadiums full of thousands at a time and millions of people in his lifetime and inspired many others to become followers of Christ. Summarize these descriptions in the column under Graham's name. Say, **Here is an example of someone who had an inspiring faith that was enhanced by his outgoing, charismatic personality.**

Next write *Jonathan Edwards* at the top of the other column and list the following descriptions underneath his name:
- *Soft-spoken preacher*
- *Read from a written manuscript*
- *Helped start a spiritual revival called the first Great Awakening*

Point out that Edwards was also successful in inspiring many, leading to a spiritual awakening that had profound impact on the church. He was used by God to inspire others with his faith, though he was not known for his charisma. Take a few minutes to acknowledge something specific about some or all of your students that is inspirational to you and could be inspirational to others.

When you are ready to move on, say, **God can use you and your unique personality to inspire others to a vibrant and growing faith.**

Option 1 (Little Prep)
Complete "My Inspirational Commitments."

Distribute copies of "My Inspirational Commitments" (Reproducible 2) and invite the students to prayerfully and personally complete each statement. Say, **Often when we make commitments such as these, we forget that we can't be successful on our own.** Close the session in a time of silent prayer during which your students ask God to help them follow through on the commitments they have made.

Finish Line

· ·

Option 2 (More Prep)
Mail yourself a note.

Distribute paper and pens or pencils and invite the students to make lists of things they might do to inspire others in their faith over the coming week. Say, **At the bottom of the list, write in bold and large letters which thing you will choose to follow through on before returning to class next week.** Ask the students to sign their commitments. Furnish stamped envelopes for the students to put their signed commitments in; the students should then self-address these envelopes. Collect the envelopes and mail them to your students later in the week so that they can be reminded of their commitments. Say, **Here is an opportunity to hold yourself accountable in your effort to inspire others around you by living out an authentic and compelling faith.**

Close the session in a time of silent prayer during which your students ask God to help them follow through on the commitments they have made.

Note:
Don't forget to distribute copies of the Portable Sanctuary to students before they leave.

NOTES

REPRODUCIBLE 1

Who Am I?

Current President or Prime Minister	Your Sunday school teacher	Your pastor or youth pastor	SpongeBob SquarePants
Dora the Explorer	Elsa from *Frozen*	Scooby Doo	Bugs Bunny
Dog	Bear	Shark	Starfish
Tiger	Snake	Caterpillar	Seagull

My Inspirational Commitment

I promise to … _____

Never will I … _____

Someday I hope to be … _____

Participating in school, I will try to be … _____

I will influence others in a positive way by … _____

Responding counter to the norm in my friendship circle, I will … ___

Around those at work, I hope to … _____

The way I will use my time … _____

In spite of negative peer pressure, I will … _____

One thing I would like to change is … _____

No temptation will … _____

As I relate with my family, I will … _____

Love will be my motivation for … _____

Portable Sanctuary

Day 1
Idol Talk

Oftentimes when I am in a texting conversation with someone else, I get frustrated with the lack of clarity and the frequency of meaningless comments. Short responses such as "Fine" to questions such as "How is your day?" do not really contribute to an in-depth relationship. The convenience factor of texting is great, but sometimes it's not enough to keep me texting. I need to talk more in depth about what's really going on. I need to hear it and speak it.

Questions and Suggestions

- Read Ezekiel 14:1–8. Does it sound as if God's people really wanted to hear from God? Why or why not? Are there times when we inquire of but are not really willing to hear an answer and be changed by it?
- Take time to thank God that he wants to recapture your heart even when you do not take the time to go deep with him.

Day 2
Eager to Do Good?

I am what could be considered a "fair weather" golfer. When the cold and wet days come, I am not terribly excited to get out on the course and hit around the little white ball. However, on the days when the sun is shining and the wind has died down, I will make every attempt to get away from my schedule and hit a round or two. The pull to the course on those days seems irresistible. But there are some golfers who are strongly drawn to the game—rain or shine. What things have an incredible pull on you?

- Read Titus 2:11–15. What is it that teaches the Christian to say no to ungodliness? Are there some ungodly things in your life you have failed to say no to?
- Ask God to redeem you from all wickedness and give you an eagerness to do what is good in God's sight.

Day 3
The Example

The other day my two-year-old son, Aaron, was playing outside with his toy hammer. He was pounding on some project that none of us were sure about when out of his mouth we heard the words, "Stupid hammer!" All of a sudden my recent golf game came to mind. I thought about when I had hit the ball off course and had commented on the lack of intelligence of the golf club I had just swung—"Stupid club!" I was reminded again that, like it or not, I am an example to others.

Questions and Suggestions

- Read 1 Corinthians 10:23—11:1. Are there things you do that you and others should not be doing? Are there things you have done or tried because of someone else's bad example? What is God saying to you about any actions he would like you to reconsider or forfeit?
- Pray and ask God to give you the strength to be a good example to others today.

Day 4
Follow the Leader

I had a friend in high school whom I looked up to quite a bit. He was fun to be around, we had much in common, and I was very impressed by how real he was in the expression and practice of his faith. After high school, he talked with me about going on a missions trip with YWAM. Within a year I found myself on mission in Jamaica. During high school I never realized that I would follow this person's leadership or that he was having a fantastic influence on my life. My time on the missions trip gave me a much wider perspective on how God is working in this world.

Questions and Suggestions

- Read Hebrews 13:1–7. Are there any leaders you remember who have influenced your life in very positive ways? Are there leaders who have influenced you in negative ways? What type of leader are *you* in the lives of your friends?
- Ask God to give you the courage and the opportunity to lead someone closer to him today.

Day 5
Snap!

I was quite involved as a swimmer in my younger years. As a matter of fact, I almost made it to lifeguard status. I have great respect for the students in my own youth group who have completed their training and worked as lifeguards in various settings. One unfortunate experience most swimmers have shared is being snapped by a towel in the locker room. Not a good feeling! I am sure there are better things to do with towels than that.

Questions and Suggestions

- Read John 13:3–15. Have you ever participated in washing someone's feet? What about washing someone's car? Jesus encouraged us to serve others and demonstrated how important this was to him. Take the opportunity today to surprise someone and serve him or her in an unexpected way.

Leading into the Session

Warm Up

Option 1 Participate in a balancing challenge.
LITTLE PREP

Option 2 Play Balderdash.
MORE PREP *Balderdash game, or word list with definitions*

Starting Line

Option 1 Write a story.
YOUNGER YOUTH *Paper, pens or pencils*

Option 2 Choose your pleasure.
OLDER YOUTH *Bible, Reproducible 2, red and green writing utensils*

Leading through the Session

Straight Away

Explore the Bible passage.
Bibles

The Turn

Perform a skit.

Leading beyond the Session

Home Stretch

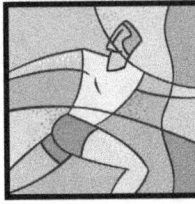

Option 1 Rewrite marriage vows.
YOUNGER YOUTH *Reproducible 2, pens or pencils*

Option 2 Create a commitment prayer.
OLDER YOUTH *Chalkboard or dry erase board*

Finish Line

Option 1 Give a gift.
LITTLE PREP *Paper, pens or pencils*

Option 2 Do a service project.
MORE PREP *Time, permission, and plans for a class service project*

SESSION 2

PLEASING TO GOD

Bible Passage
1 Thessalonians 2

Key Verse
We had previously suffered and been insulted in Philippi, as you know, but with the help of our God we dared to tell you his gospel in spite of strong opposition.
—1 Thessalonians 2:2

Main Thought
Our lives should be motivated by a commitment to please God.

Bible Background

In modern Western culture, it is not unusual for individuals to be urged to set and to strive to achieve certain goals. At times it seems to matter little what those goals might be. A young woman who practices long hours to become a professional basketball player, a businessman who seeks to increase his company's profits, or a musician who endeavors to master a musical instrument and play in Carnegie Hall might all be equally lauded by others for their discipline in setting and diligently working to realize their goals.

And, certainly, there is something commendable about a commitment that is focused and coupled with discipline and hard work. In the second chapter of Thessalonians, however, the Apostle Paul pointed to what he considered to be the supreme commitment of them all—a commitment to please God.

Paul began this portion of the letter by defending his ministry among the Thessalonians. As was often the case, Paul seemed to have had detractors who were attacking him. Apparently some had accused him of having "impure motives" or using trickery as he worked to bring the Thessalonians to the place where they would accept the gospel (1 Thess 2:3).

In responding to his critics, Paul sought to clarify his goals and make it equally clear who he was laboring to please. As he plainly put it in verse 4, "We are not trying to please men [or women] but God, who tests our hearts."

In characterizing his work, and that of his companions, he used two parental images to underscore his motives and the gentle, loving care he demonstrated toward the believers in the fellowship in Thessalonica. He and the others were "gentle…, like a mother caring for her little children" (v 7) and they dealt with the people "as a father deals with his own children" (v 11). These were not the actions of individuals who were seeking their own gain or glory.

In all they did, in other words, Paul and his fellow apostles sought to do what they had been called to do by God. They did this so that the Thessalonians, in turn, might "live lives worthy of God" (v 12). It was Paul's goal to encourage the Thessalonians, by example and exhortation, to reflect God's character in their daily lives. Like the Israelites, they were being called to be holy because God is holy (Lev 19:2). They were being called to make pleasing God their highest priority.

Leading into the Session

Option 1 (Little Prep)
Participate in a balancing challenge.

Invite the class members to participate in a balance and strength challenge. The students should pair up and stand face-to-face, about two feet apart, palms facing one another. Placing their palms against those of their opponent, the object is to push on the opponent's palms, forcing him or her to lose balance and move his or her feet. Play "best of three" and then match the winners up for another best of three. Continue in this fashion until you have a victor.

Say, **When we face opposition, we must have strength and commitment in order to overcome the opposition.**

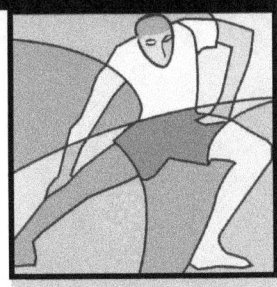

WARM UP

Note:
If you sent the Portable Sanctuary home with students last week, take some time at the beginning of this session to review and discuss their experience.

Option 2 (More Prep)
Play Balderdash.

Bring to class a copy of the Balderdash game or your own list of odd words and their definitions. The purpose of the game is to make up a correct-sounding definition for a word and to trick your classmates into voting for your definition. The word is read and the players each make up a definition. Then the players vote on which definition they think is the correct one. After the votes are tallied, provide the correct definition. A player gets three points for each vote for his or her definition and receives two points for actually identifying the correct definition. Play as many rounds as time allows, tally up the points, and declare a winner. Ask, **What was your main goal as you made up definitions for the words?** The motive was to mislead or misguide the others into voting for their incorrect definitions. They were not trying to teach the real meaning of the words to their classmates. The motive was deception, not truth.

Say, **There are motives behind everything we do. Sometimes the motives are good, and sometimes they're not so good.**

Option 1 (Younger Youth)
Write a story.

Say, **You are all going to tag team as a class and co-author a short story.** Write at the top of a sheet of paper, *Ethan was faced with a dilemma when his friends asked him, "Have you bought your new purple tuxedo for the formal dinner yet?"* Hand the paper to one student, who should add one sentence, fold the paper back so that all the preceding lines except for the one just written are hidden, and pass the paper on to the next person, who should write a line and fold the paper back before passing it, and so forth. After the story has made its rounds, read it aloud. Invite your students to share whether they tried to write lines that fit the story or purposely tried to create an odd tale.

When you are ready to move on, say, **Let's see what the Apostle Paul said about fitting in with others.**

STARTING LINE

Note:
Depending on time available and class size, you could select a group of volunteers to participate, or start several papers at once.

21

Option 2 (Older Youth)
Choose your pleasure.

Distribute copies of "Choose Your Pleasure" (Reproducible 1) and red and green writing utensils (markers, crayons, or colored pencils). Ask the students to read the list. They should circle in green those things that would please God, circle in red those things that would not please God, and circle in both colors those things that could go either way. After allowing time to complete the handout, discuss responses. Spend some time exploring the concept that for the children of God "all things are permissible, but not all things are beneficial" (see 1 Corinthians 10:23). Talk also about the importance of the motives behind our actions (see Isaiah 1:13–17 and 1 Corinthians 10:31). Point out that even something such as church attendance can be less than pleasing to God depending on why it is done.

When you are ready to move on, say, **Let's see what the Apostle Paul had to say to his friends in Thessalonica about their motives.**

Leading through the Session

STRAIGHT AWAY

Explore the Bible passage.

Read together 1 Thessalonians 2 (the whole chapter) and discuss the following questions:

- **What was it that made Paul's visit to the Thessalonian church a success?** He and his companions dared to present the gospel in spite of the strong opposition they were faced with. Point out that oftentimes when presenting the gospel we tend to base our success or failure on the response of the hearer. It is important for us to remember that we are responsible for sharing, but we are not responsible for the response of those with whom we are sharing. If they fail to receive the message, we have not necessarily failed.

- **What made Paul so sure that his motives and those of his companions were pure?** They were not trying to please people but God; they were not trying to trick, did not use flattery, and were not motivated by greed. If someone who is sharing about God is glad to get our personal praise, has to lie to get us to listen, tries to butter us up with overused compliments, or is eager to get paid, we are right to question that person's motives.

- **What is the difference between how people "test" one another and how God tests us?** Be sure your students understand that "test" here refers to discerning one's motives and not displaying one's algebra skills! People look at the outside, at actions and words, considering measurable results to try to determine motives. God looks at the heart, going straight to the motives.

- **How could Paul and his fellow evangelists have been a "burden" to the Thessalonian church?** The contrasting statements in this paragraph make it clear that they were gentle (instead of harsh), happy (instead of hesitant) to share the gospel and their own lives, and willing to work to feed and take care of themselves (instead of just living off their hosts the whole time).

- **If Paul and his fellow ministers were not paid, why do you think that we pay our pastors and ministers in the church today?** Encourage a lively discussion among the students and draw their attention to other Bible passages that infrom this topic (e.g., Deuteronomy 25:4; Luke 10:7; 1 Timothy 5:18, and so forth).

- **What analogies of ministry did Paul use in this passage?** He said that it was "like a mother caring for her little children" and like a father who encourages, comforts, and urges his own children. Paul also referred to the recipients of the letter as his brothers. This was a close relationship, and Paul cared deeply about these people.
- **What is the difference between accepting the word of people and the word of God?** The word of people can definitely benefit us (e.g., the guiding and protecting words of our parents or the wise words of our teachers). However, the word of God has eternal benefits. The word of God works in us to change us and to change others.
- **What did Paul mean here about the "wrath of God" (v 16)?** When Paul's friends at Thessalonica accepted Christ, they were rejected by their fellow citizens. These people were not just rejecting Christians, they were rejecting their own opportunity to know God. To accept God's invitation to a relationship is to accept his mercy; to reject it is to invite his wrath.

Say, **Paul praised his friends in Thessalonica for their commitment to serve and please God.**

Perform a skit.
Say, **I want to give you an opportunity to direct and perfrom your very own comedic play.** Invite the students to use tools such as humor and exaggeration to depict a mother caring for her little children and an encouraging, comforting, and urging father dealing with his children. Allow your group members to prepare the presentation for you and then perform it. Emphasize the power of these illustrations how Paul, Silas, and Timothy ministered to their friends in the Thessalonian church. Be sensitive to any students who come from rough home environments and do not experience this kind of parenting.

Say, **Our Father God encourages, urges, and comforts us with a deep and eternal love.**

The Turn

Note:
Depending on your time and size of your class, either have everyone perform, involve a few volunteers, or involve groups of volunteers.

Leading beyond the Session

Option 1 (Younger Youth)
Rewrite marriage vows.
Distribute copies of "Rewrite the Vows" (Reproducible 2). Invite the students to read the sets of marriage vows and to take some time to write their own vows, focusing on the commitment they want to make or have made with God. Encourage the class members to sign and date the handout when they are through. Invite those who might be making a new or first-time commitment to Christ to speak with you more in depth following your class time.

When you are ready to move on, say, **As we make and live out these kinds of commitments, God is pleased with us.**

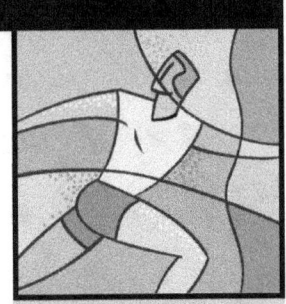

Home Stretch

Option 2 (Older Youth)
Create a commitment prayer.

Work together as a class to write a prayer of commitment based on the Bible passage and concepts you have discussed today. Give the students an opportunity to contribute ideas as you write their thoughts on the board. After you have compiled the finished product, read it aloud together. If you wish, you can ask the students to write it down and take it home, or you can send it to them later in the week.

When you are ready to move on, say, **Recommitting ourselves to serve God should be something we do every day of our lives.**

Finish Line

Option 1 (Little Prep)
Give a gift.

Say, **Gifts can bring joy to the ones who receive them and the ones who give them.** Distribute paper and pens or pencils and invite the students to write short notes that they can later give as gifts to their father, mother, or a sibling. The notes should represent gifts through promised acts of service (e.g., I will wash and detail our family vehicle this week, I will cook a meal, I will do the dishes, I will clean a room, I will do the laundry, I will complete a certain chore, and so forth). Ask the students to give these promissory gifts to the people of their choice today. Say, **This will not only bless the recipient, but it will bless you and bless God if you give it in love and follow through with your promise.**

Close the session in prayer.

Note:
Don't forget to distribute copies of the Portable Sanctuary to students before they leave.

Option 2 (More Prep)
Do a service project.

Beforehand, prepare a project requiring some hard work that your class can take part in. Some examples could include sweeping the church parking lots, washing some walls, cleaning the church restrooms, washing some church windows, mopping some kitchen floors, weeding the church flowerbeds, and so forth. Say, **Hard work is a value the Apostle Paul spoke of. Today I have made arrangements for us to get a little taste of some hard work as we serve the church family we are a part of.** Encourage the students to think about their motivation for the project and invite them to pray before working, asking God to help them to work out of a desire to please him, not simply because that is what you as a teacher are instructing. After the task is accomplished, be sure to thank the students and perhaps seek out a way for them to receive some public acknowledgment for their work if you feel that is appropriate.

Choose Your Pleasure

Look at the objects below. Circle in green those things that would please God, circle in red those things that would not please God, and circle in both colors those things that could go either way.

REPRODUCIBLE 2

Rewrite the Vows

Read the sets of classic marriage vows written below, then take some time to design your own vows, focusing on the commitment you want to make or have made with God. When you are finished, sign and date at the bottom.

I, (name), take you, (name), to be my lawfully wedded (husband/wife). In the presence of

_____

God, my family, and my friends, I promise to love you and care for you in joy and in

_____

sorrow, in sickness and in health, as long as we both shall live. I accept you with all your

_____

flaws and strengths as I offer myself to you with my own weaknesses and strengths. I

_____

promise to help, cherish, support, and love you unconditionally throughout my life. I

_____

choose you as the person with whom I want to spend the rest of my days.

_____

I, (name), take you, (name), to be my (husband/wife) from this day forward. In the

_____

presence of God and these witnesses, I promise you to be your true partner in sickness

_____

and in health, in joy and in sorrow. I will always love, honor, and respect you until death

_____

do us part.

_____

Today, in the presence of my family and friends I, (name), take you, (name), to be my

_____

lawfully wedded (husband/wife), my true friend, my faithful partner, and my eternal love,

_____

from this day forward until my last breath.

_____

_____

_____ _____
signature   *date*

Portable Sanctuary

Day 1
Sent with Power

I recently had the experience of being sent on a mission on behalf of my wife. We had booked a hotel room and found that the shower had no hot water. This was not a good situation. My wife sent me to the front desk to have a conversation with the manager. Now normally I am hesitant to rock the boat. If I had been staying alone, I would have probably just lived with the cold water. Not in this case. I was sent. Having my wife to send made my talk with the manager much easier. Sometimes knowing that we are sent and the power of the one who sent us can provide great motivation.

Questions and Suggestions

- Read Galatians 1:1–10. Have you ever been sent by someone to do something on his or her behalf? What has God sent you to do today, and to whom has he sent you?
- Approach this day encouraged that you are sent by God, your Creator and Lord.

Day 2
Character Counts

I was golfing with a friend the other day and he hit a ball deep into the trees. I knew he was hitting a Callaway-brand ball, so I quickly pulled one out of my bag and went to help him find his lost ball. I set the ball I had taken out in a place where I thought he could easily hit it out of the trees and hollered, "Are you hitting a Callaway?" He came running and thanked me for finding his ball. After finishing the hole, I said, "That was a great find!" My friend laughed and said, "I know this is a ball from your bag. My Callaway did not have the advertising logo on it." So much for my clever prank.

NOTES

Questions and Suggestions

- Read Acts 17:10–14. Would you say that you are of noble character? Why or why not? Do you consider closely what others say to find out whether or not you are being told the truth?
- Ask God to keep you attentive to the truth and what his Word, the Bible, is saying to you.

Day 3
Seek and You Will Find

A couple of years ago I began looking for a replacement for my old car. I set my heart on a brand-new Camaro convertible. I wanted a black one with the eight-cylinder motor, a five-speed manual transmission, and leather interior. I looked and looked and looked. After a few months my wife asked me what was taking so long. She may have thought that I was being a little stubborn or even overzealous in my search. But after a few more months of hard looking, I came across the car I wanted. It even had a few extras!

Questions and Suggestions

- Read Hebrews 11:4–7. Have you ever searched high and low and then not found the item you were looking for? How did that make you feel? After a long, hard search have you ever found the thing you never expected you would be able to find? How did you feel about that?
- Thank God that he is true to his word and that you can find him when you are earnestly seeking.

Day 4
Say It or Show It

The other day my two-year-old son said, "I love you, Dad." Then within a couple of minutes, he got angry and hauled off and hit me. Later on I was getting ready to barbeque for supper. Without my even asking, my five-year-old son brought me my barbeque tools and some other things he knew I would need to finish the job. Which one of these boys do you think I felt more loved by? Definitely my older son. Although he did not say the words, what he did showed me that he loved me. Either that or he was *really* hungry.

Questions and Suggestions

- Read 1 John 3:18–24. Have you ever said the words, "I love you," out loud to your Heavenly Father? What have you done recently to show God that you love him?
- Right now, shout out loud to God, "I love you!" Now ask him to give you an opportunity today to show your love to him by what you do.

Day 5
Missing You

This past weekend I spent time away from my children. I did quite a few enjoyable things and my days were quite full. In spite of this, I could not help but think about my three boys and what they might be up to in my absence. After the first day went by, I broke down and gave them a call. I found out that all three were sick. What a bum deal. The rest of the weekend I kept thinking of them and looking forward to getting home so I could give them a big daddy-type hug. Have you ever missed someone you cared for a whole lot?

Questions and Suggestions

- Read 1 Thessalonians 2:17–20. Why do you think Paul missed the Thessalonians so much? Do you sometimes feel that Satan wants to keep people away from you who give you joy?
- Thank God that he is more powerful than the enemy of your soul and ask him to make your joy complete when you find yourself separated from those you care for.

Leading into the Session

Warm Up

Option 1 Complete a challenge.
LITTLE PREP *Bible or other heavy book*
Option 2 Watch a video clip.
MORE PREP *Movie Facing the Giants and the equipment to view it*

Starting Line

Option 1 Search the Scriptures.
YOUNGER YOUTH *Bible, concordance*
Option 2 Do a word study.
OLDER YOUTH *Dictionary, thesaurus*

Leading through the Session

Straight Away

Explore the Bible passage.
Bibles

The Turn

Put it in context.
Bibles, Reproducible 1, pens or pencils

Leading beyond the Session

Home Stretch

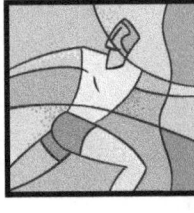

Option 1 Encourage one another.
YOUNGER YOUTH *Paper, tape, markers*
Option 2 Write prayers.
OLDER YOUTH *Chalkboard or dry erase board, paper, pens or pencils*

Finish Line

Option 1 Prepare for an encouragement
LITTLE PREP assignment.
Reproducible 2, pens or pencils
Option 2 Write encouragement cards.
MORE PREP *Encouragement cards, envelopes, pens, pencils, markers*

SESSION 3

AN ENCOURAGING FAITH

Bible Passage
1 Thessalonians 3

Key Verse
In all our distress and persecution we were encouraged about you because of your faith. —1 Thessalonians 3:7

Main Thought
Giving and receiving encouragement strengthens our faith.

Bible Background

Jesus was resurrected from the dead and had been seen by many believers who were still living in the time of Paul. Prior to his ascension, Jesus had promised to return. Wherever Paul brought the gospel, he taught new believers about the crucified, resurrected, and soon-to-return Lord. The ancient church lived on tiptoe in the expectation of the Lord's imminent return, and this hope sustained the church throughout numerous trials and adversities. Inevitably, the seeming delay of Christ's return raised questions in the minds of believers. Increased persecution lent an even greater urgency. In the face of hostility and the persecution of his church, why did the Lord tarry? The lack of a ready answer to that question sometimes threatened to undermine hope, and Paul wanted to prevent such a loss among the Thessalonians. For that reason, as he put it to the Thessalonian believers, Paul sent Timothy to "encourage you in your faith, so that no one would be unsettled by these trials" (1 Thess 3:2–3). Though Paul wanted to encourage the Thessalonians, he did not paint an unrealistically rosy picture of what they faced. When he had been with them in previous times, he had been blunt in telling them that those who followed Christ were "destined" (v 3) to face persecution. Rather than telling them that their persecutions would soon end, he prayed that God would strengthen their hearts (v 13). While Paul had sent Timothy to encourage the Thessalonians, he also found himself heartened by what Timothy had found. The believers in Thessalonica were standing firm in the faith. In addition to expressing his joy in their faithfulness, Paul prayed that the Thessalonians' love might "increase and overflow for each other and for everyone else" (v 12). If hope is the Christian virtue oriented especially to the future and Christ's return, faith and love are the virtues to be displayed in the meantime. It will not do for Christians to hope in a manner that allows them to wait idly. There is work to be done in the meantime. Paul knew that it is faith that yields work, and our labors are prompted by love. Love is a social virtue; it defines and supports our relationships. But Paul also regarded faith as an active virtue that implies connections with others. The Thessalonians might be facing persecution, but faith and love were alive and well and the source of much well-doing.

Leading into the Session

Option 1 (Little Prep)
Complete a challenge.

Challenge the students to make an effort to lie on their backs and hold their feet six inches above the ground, without bending their knees, while balancing a Bible upon their ankles. Allow each student to make an attempt while the other students sit quietly looking the other way. Time the efforts for comparative purposes. After each student has had the opportunity to try one time, invite them all to try one more time. This time allow their peers to encourage them and cheer them on as they try to beat the times they previously scored. In most cases they will likely improve their scores with the additional encouragement they receive from their peers.

Say, **Encouragement can make all the difference when we are trying to complete a difficult or challenging task.**

WARM UP

Note:
If you sent the Portable Sanctuary home with students last week, take some time at the beginning of this session to review and discuss their experience.

Option 2 (More Prep)
Watch a video clip.

Show your students the "death crawl" scene (Scene 12) from the movie *Facing the Giants*. Show the video up to the point where the coach is encouraging Brock to use the God-given gift of leadership that he has to motivate the team to win against their more challenging opponents. After showing the clip, point out how beneficial encouragement can be. Because of the coach's focused encouragement, Brock went from an already defeated attitude to realizing the great potential he had to go farther than he had ever gone before.

Say, **Encouragement can make all the difference when we are trying to complete a difficult or challenging task.**

Note:
This entire movie would be very appropriate and beneficial to share with your students.

Option 1 (Younger Youth)
Search the Scriptures.

Furnish Bibles and a concordance and ask the students to spend some time looking up passages relating to encouragement. Some possible passages to use include 2 Samuel 19:7; Isaiah 1:17; Acts 15:32; Romans 12:8; Titus 2:6; Hebrews 3:13; and Colossians 2:2. Briefly discuss each passage that is identified and what the verses have to teach us about encouragement. Point out that encouraging one another is a very important part of a growing faith. There are many passages in the Bible that remind us of the importance of encouragement.

When you are ready to move on, say, **Let's see how Paul set out to encourage his friends—and was himself encouraged.**

STARTING LINE

Option 2 (Older Youth)
Do a word study.

Utilizing a dictionary and a thesaurus, work together as a class to study the word *encouragement*. Point out that the heart of the word centers on *courage*; the word can be defined as "giving courage." Invite the students to contribute their own ideas and examples in addition to those you look up. Ask, **In light of this word study, what should encouragement look like? What type of an effect will it most often have on a person?** Invite the students to respond.

When you are ready to move on, say, **Let's see how Paul set out to encourage his friends—and was himself encouraged.**

Leading through the Session

STRAIGHT AWAY

Explore the Bible passage.

Read together 1 Thessalonians 3 (the whole chapter) and discuss the following questions:

- **Why do you think Paul was concerned that the trials the Thessalonians were facing would unsettle them or cause them to lose faith?** Oftentimes as people face difficulties or trials the first thing they do is blame God or question God for not rescuing them. Some people walk away from the faith rather than looking to God who has promised to never leave or forsake us.

- **Why are Christians sometimes surprised when they run into trials?** Unfortunately, there has been some false teaching in the church that has led some to believe that walking with God will eliminate all the troubles we face in this world. Remind the students that, contrary to this false teaching, in order to follow God we must "take up" our own "cross" (Matthew 16:24); this is not always an easy or enjoyable task. We will have trouble in this world even when we serve God. Paul did not want to keep the Thessalonians in the dark about the persecution they would face.

- **What or who is often the cause of someone's loss of faith in the midst of trials?** Paul pointed out that this is often due to "the tempter" (Satan) himself who will go to any measure to cause us to lose our faith. One could also make a successful argument that false teaching or misinterpreting of the Scriptures can also lead to this end result. Sometimes we ourselves are to blame as we look for reasons to cave and do what comes easier, following our sinful nature.

- **Who else sometimes gets the blame for our questioning or leaving our faith?** Accept other reasonable answers, but point out that other people are often the recipients of blame when we don't want to take responsibility for our own bad choices. For example, if the Thessalonians had decided to give up on God during their trials and persecution, they could have blamed Paul for leaving them or his teaching for falling short, or they could have blamed those who were persecuting them instead of acknowledging their own freedom of choice in the matter. Use this question as an opportunity to remind the students that God loves them so much he is willing to give them a choice as to whether or not they will live lives of faith.

- **What was the result of the positive report that Timothy brought back to Paul regarding the Thessalonian church?** Paul was greatly encouraged by their faithfulness. Their faith influenced him to continue on in his own faith with renewed vigor and excitement in spite of the persecution and distress he was facing.

- **Can our memories serve an important role in our faith? Why or why not?** Accept reasonable answers. Draw attention to the fact that the positive memories that Paul shared with the Thessalonians continued to draw them both together and strengthen each of them in their faith. Also mention that throughout the Bible God reminded his people, and they reminded one another, of what God had done for them in the past. Oftentimes such memories carry us through difficult times when it may seem that God has let us down.
- **What memories do you have that encourage your own faith?** Allow the students to share about important experiences in their faith journeys that serve this purpose for them. Some memories might center on camp, baptism, the salvation experience, a missions trip, and so forth.
- **What role did Paul continue to play in the lives of the Thessalonians in spite of the reality that they were separated from him by a great distance? What can this example encourage us to remember?** Even across the miles, Paul continued to give thanks for what God had done in his friends' lives and to pray for their continued growth in the faith. Paul's example can lead us to do the same for those we know who are striving to grow in faith. We may even want to consider following precisely Paul's example and to pray the words that Paul prayed in verses 12 and 13 on behalf of our own brothers and sisters who may need encouragement in the faith.

Say, **As Paul and his friends gave and received encouragement, their faith was strengthened.**

The Turn

Put it in context.

Distribute copies of "Put It in Context" (Reproducible 1) or show it as a projection, go over the instructions, and allow time for the students to complete the handout. Suggested answers are as follows:

- He went to the synagogue to preach.
- Jews, God-fearing Greeks, and prominent women.
- A riot.
- Jason's house.
- They sent Paul and Silas to Berea to help the two remain safe.
- The angry Jews, to stir up trouble.
- To the coast (Athens).

Answers should demonstrate an understanding of what took place in this narrative.

Point out that it is helpful to know the reasons why Paul left the Thessalonians in the first place, and the things that they had already been through together.

Say, **Paul was not just making up some nice words when he wrote to his friends; he really did miss them and wanted to return to build upon the relationships he had started and encourage the faith that had begun when he was with them before.**

Leading beyond the Session

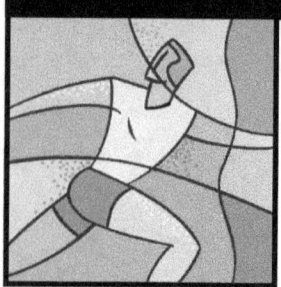

HOME STRETCH

Option 1 (Younger Youth)
Encourage one another.

Tape a sheet of paper to each student's back. Distribute markers and invite the students to make their way around the room, writing at least one encouraging thing on the back of each person who is in class. Challenge them, if they are able, to go deeper than clichéd, "Your-hair-looks-great" types of comments. After the comments are written, allow time for the students to remove their papers and read them.

When you are ready to move on, say, **It often takes time and effort to encourage others. Sometimes put-downs and negative comments seem to flow more quickly.**

Note:
Experiment to make sure you use paper and markers that do not allow the markers to bleed through.

· ·

Option 2 (Older Youth)
Write prayers.

Utilizing the chalkboard or dry erase board, brainstorm together a list of things that you and your students appreciate about your church family. Also take the time to list some things that you would like to see God do more of among the members of your congregation. Using these lists, invite your students to write their own prayers that thank God for what he is doing and has done in your church family. Also include in the prayers some requests regarding some of the things you would like to see God do more of among your youth group. If possible, make arrangements to share these prayers with the rest of the congregation.

When you are ready to move on, say, **God can move us beyond just speaking with him about these matters to encouraging others to be open to the things God would like to do among us.**

FINISH LINE

Option 1 (Little Prep)
Prepare for an encouragement assignment.

Distribute copies of "Encouragement Assignment" (Reproducible 2) to the students. Ask them take some time to look at the list and write down specific ways they might encourage these people. Also invite them to fill in names in the *other* category if any come to mind. Challenge the students to take the time in the coming week to encourage as many of these people as they are able. As they make a specific effort to encourage someone, they should put a check mark in the appropriate box.

Close by praying together with the students, asking God to bless their efforts as they endeavor to encourage those they come in contact with in the coming week.

Option 2 (More Prep)
Write encouragement cards.

Bring to class an assortment of encouragement cards, envelopes, pens, pencils, and markers. Invite the students to take the time to write a few notes of encouragement to those they know who may be in need of some encouragement. Suggest to the students that they think "outside the box" of people they might not interact with very often. If you focus on church members, you can distribute your notes following class. Say, **Sometimes a simple card can brighten a person's day much more than we might think.**

Close the session in prayer.

> *Note:*
> Don't forget to distribute copies of the Portable Sanctuary to students before they leave.

NOTES

REPRODUCIBLE 1

Put It in Context

Read Acts 17:1–15.

1. What was Paul's custom when he visited a town?
   _____

2. What three types of people were persuaded by Paul's reasoning in Thessalonica?
   _____

3. What dangerous event followed Paul's presentation?
   _____

4. Where did the mob go to look for Paul?
   _____

5. Where did the believers send Paul and Silas that night and why did they send them there?
   _____

6. Who followed them to Berea, and why?
   _____

7. Where did the believers send Paul next?
   _____

8. In your own words, why did Paul leave Thessalonica?
   _____

REPRODUCIBLE 2

Encouragement Assignment

This week, how could you provide specific encouragement to the people listed below? There is space to add other categories you might think of. As you actually provide encouragement to a person, check the appropriate box.

FAMILY
- ☐ Father _____
- ☐ Mother _____
- ☐ Brother _____
- ☐ Sister _____
- ☐ Other _____

SCHOOL
- ☐ Principal _____
- ☐ Teacher _____
- ☐ Custodian _____
- ☐ Vice Principal _____
- ☐ Secretary _____
- ☐ Friend _____
- ☐ Other _____

WORKPLACE
- ☐ Boss _____
- ☐ Co-worker _____
- ☐ Other _____

CONGREGATION
- ☐ Piano player _____
- ☐ Senior pastor _____
- ☐ Janitor _____
- ☐ Sunday school teacher _____
- ☐ Nursery worker _____
- ☐ Usher _____
- ☐ Greeter _____
- ☐ Elder _____
- ☐ Secretary _____
- ☐ Song leader _____
- ☐ Other _____

ANY OTHER PLACES OR PEOPLE
- ☐ _____
- ☐ _____
- ☐ _____

Portable Sanctuary

Day 1
The Benefits of a Mentor

I have an older gentleman in my life whom I consider a mentor. He and I meet on a regular basis to discuss many things. We talk about my job, my role in my family, and my walk with Christ. We talk about more personal matters and my own practice of the spiritual disciplines. These meetings can sometimes prove to be a bit scary, for I know there are many areas where I have fallen short and can use growth. One thing that I really appreciate about my mentor is that he is an encourager. Although he does not hesitate to ask me the hard questions and challenge me, I know that I will leave our time together feeling encouraged rather than discouraged, built up rather than cut down.

Questions and Suggestions

- Read Acts 4:32–37. What is the meaning of the name *Barnabas*? What is a great example of the type of thing he did for encouragement? Would someone ever call *you* a son or daughter of encouragement? Why or why not?
- Ask God to make you an encouragement to someone today.

Day 2
God Provides

I was talking with a friend of mine the other day whom I went to college with. After college, we both headed to get our master's degrees. I was able to finish mine off, but after a few semesters my friend gave up. As we were talking the other day, I learned that my friend's current job pays more than three times what I am currently making. I was quite happy for him and took some time to encourage him and remind him

Questions and Suggestions

- Read Acts 18:1–11. Do you think it would have been easy for Paul to get discouraged or feel that he was all alone as he faced so much opposition to his teaching? What helpful reminder did he get from the Lord in a vision?
- Thank God that you are not alone in your own efforts to live a life that brings God glory. Ask God to make you an encouragement to others who feel alone in their Christian walk, and ask that God would bring others into your life who can do that for you.

NOTES

to be thankful for what God has provided. Some people in my shoes may have had trouble with feeling as though things were unfair in who was getting paid what.

Questions and Suggestions

- Read Deuteronomy 3:21–29. What was Moses missing out on that he was told Joshua was going to enjoy? What was the role Moses was asked by God to play in the life of his second in command, Joshua? Is there someone whose situation you may even be jealous of whom God would desire you to encourage?
- Ask God to forgive you of any jealousy and to give you the strength to be an encouragement to others.

Day 3
Good Move

I found myself a little discouraged not long ago as we went through the process of buying a new house. It seemed as though no one wanted our old house, and if they did they were not willing to pay anywhere near what it had cost us. A friend of mine who is in the real estate business had a chat with me and reminded me of the bigger picture. He encouraged me to be patient. His encouragement and optimism came at the right time. Not long after that we were able to make the move, and things have worked out to our benefit.

Questions and Suggestions

- Read Isaiah 35:1–4. Has there ever been a time when someone's timely encouragement helped you through a tough place in life? Is there someone you know who may be going through a difficult time right now?
- Ask God to open your eyes to the opportunities he has given you to help others through tough times by giving them the encouragement they need.

Day 4
Superior Strength

I was in the yard yesterday while my boys were building a fort out of various lawn toys they were gathering. They were having trouble moving one of their larger climbing structures that was going to play a key role in their design. After giving it some great effort, they ended up coming to Dad for a helping hand. I suspect someday they will be bigger and stronger than me, but in this case I was able to pull off what my three young boys could not do together. My superior strength came through for them.

Questions and Suggestions

- Read Romans 15:1–6. Whose example should we follow when it comes to helping others who are weaker than we are, not just physically but in their faith? How can you give others hope who are feeling hopeless right now?
- Say a prayer opening yourself up to help those weaker than you. Ask God to help you remain humble, especially in times when you feel that you may be stronger in faith than someone whom God is using you to encourage.

Day 5
Small-Town Blues

Sometimes the members of my youth group share with me the struggles they face living in our small town. One common concern they often express is that it seems to them that there are not very many teenagers here who are trying to live a Christian life. They feel vastly outnumbered. Once a year, though, we go to a youth convention called YC Alberta. Throughout the weekend we are able to worship, learn, and fellowship with more than 16,000 other students, most of whom are trying to live a Christian life. What an encouragement this event is to the young people in our church.

Leading into the Session

Warm Up

Option 1 — LITTLE PREP
Brainstorm about pleasing God.
Chalkboard or dry erase board

Option 2 — MORE PREP
Play spoons.
Playing cards, spoon for every student

Starting Line

Option 1 — YOUNGER YOUTH
Conduct a contest.
Marshmallows

Option 2 — OLDER YOUTH
Discuss authority.

Leading through the Session

Straight Away

Explore the Bible passage.
Bibles

The Turn

Make a list.
Bibles, chalkboard or dry erase board

Leading beyond the Session

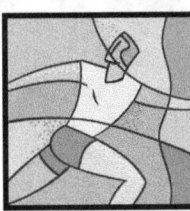

Home Stretch

Option 1 — YOUNGER YOUTH
Listen to "Shine."
Audio of the song "Shine" by the Newsboys and the necessary equipment to listen to it

Option 2 — OLDER YOUTH
Mind your own business.
Reproducible 1, pens or pencils

Finish Line

Option 1 — LITTLE PREP
Rate your work ethic.
Reproducible 2, pens or pencils

Option 2 — MORE PREP
Create symbols.
Markers, colored paper, toothpicks, glue, playdough, cardboard, rubber bands, nails, small shapes of wood, scissors, drinking straws, tacks, paper clips, and so forth

---

SESSION 4

FAITH IN ACTION

Bible Passage
1 Thessalonians 4:1–12

Key Verse
Make it your ambition to lead a quiet life, to mind your own business and to work with your hands, just as we told you.
—1 Thessalonians 4:11

Main Thought
Our faith in action can bring God pleasure.

Bible Background

Paul's first letter to the Thessalonians may have been written as early as twenty years following the resurrection of Christ. As a cradle of Christian faith, this church's history can be compacted into three small words: *potential*, *problems*, and *prayer*—words that can be applied to every church in every age.

Paul believed that he had been divinely directed to Thessalonica because of the city's potential. As a financial center, it was the hub of commerce for land and sea. As a free city, it was essentially Greek and therefore intellectually alive. In such an atmosphere of exploration and expansion, converts responded to the gospel of Christ.

Although a good response brought about the establishment of a strong church, it was not without its problems. Rapid growth, then as now, confronted the church with change, and after Paul's departure, he was informed that some problems did in fact need attention. Paul addressed each of these in his first letter: (1) Theological confusion about the resurrection (1 Thess 4:11–18). (2) Rejection of authority, with some believers questioning Paul's leadership (1 Thess 5:12–14). (3) Constant temptation for converts to return to former pagan practices of immorality (1 Thess 4:3–8). (4) Lack of discipline in accepting responsibility for the life of the local church (1 Thess 4:9; 5:13).

Solutions to such problems were not to be found in the financial or intellectual resources of the Thessalonians. Instead, Paul insisted, the answers were theological, relational, and spiritual. Repeatedly, he supported a practical theology of holiness with the words "mentioning you in our prayers" (1:2), "we pray most earnestly" (3:10), "pray continually" (5:17), and "pray for us" (5:25).

These verses sound a call to holiness. A call to personal, ethical holiness as indicated in 4:1–8 is followed by a challenge to relational holiness in the context of the community of faith (5:12–24). Personal holiness enables people to conduct their lives in ways acceptable to God. It makes possible the practice of abstinence and fidelity in moral matters of individual conduct, and integrity in all other aspects of life.

Regarding holiness as it affects our relationships within the church, Paul also reminded believers to love, cherish, and encourage one another. And should it appear to be more than we are capable of doing, in the final chapter of this letter he reminds us that God is the one who enables us to be holy.

Leading into the Session

WARM UP

Option 1 (Little Prep)
Brainstorm about pleasing God.

Ask, **What kinds of things can we do in order to please God?** Invite the students to brainstorm answers to this question as you write their responses on the board. Some possible suggestions might include pray, read the Bible, go to church, love God and love others, care for the needy, and similar things. Point out that there are many different things we can do to please God.

Say, **Pleasing God is not rocket science; God's Word gives us many examples of what we can do to please God.**

. . . .

Option 2 (More Prep)
Play Spoons.

Bring to class a deck of Skip-Bo cards (numbers only) and one spoon for each student. Have the students sit around a table or in a circle on the floor with all the spoons in the middle, minus one. Depending on the time available and the size of the group, you can play this game in one of two ways:

- Deal four cards to everyone. One player draws a card from the remainder of the deck and then discards one card to the player on the right, who picks that card up and discards one to the right, and so forth. The object is to get four cards of a kind (e.g., four twos). If your class is large, you might divide into multiple small groups and furnish a deck for each group.
- Instead of dealing any cards, flip up one card at a time so that the students can see it. The object is to look for a specific card to be revealed.

When a player gets four of a kind or when you flip up a certain designated card, everyone tries to snag one spoon from the middle. Whichever student is left without a spoon is out, after which another round is conducted. (Be sure to remove another spoon after each round.) When only one student is left, bring everyone back into the game and play again. This time take out any player who flinches or reaches at the wrong time, as well as the person left without a spoon when the spoons are grabbed. Explain that in this game, the person who has the greatest amount of self-control has a huge advantage over those who reach every time.

Say, **Self-control is not only beneficial to us, but it is also pleasing to God.**

Note:
If you sent the Portable Sanctuary home with students last week, take some time at the beginning of this session to review and discuss their experience.

STARTING LINE

Option 1 (Younger Youth)
Conduct a contest.

Bring to class a good supply of marshmallows and conduct a contest to see who can use the most marshmallows to complete a certain task. Here are some possibilities:

- Who can cram the largest number of marshmallows into a cup or other limited space?
- Who can carry the most marshmallows across the room without dropping any?

43

- Who can shoot the most marshmallows into a wastebasket from across the room?

Point out that with marshmallows, it is often possible to find room for more and more. In life, there is often room for us to do more things that will please the Lord.

When you are ready to move on, say, **Let's see what the Apostle Paul had to say to his friends about how they were living for the Lord and about how they could do so more and more.**

. . . .

Option 2 (Older Youth)
Discuss authority.

Ask the students a number of questions to get them thinking about authorities they have in their lives. As the teacher, be sure that you also answer these questions from your own perspective, making the students aware that even as an adult you must acknowledge authority figures in your life:

- **Who is the authority in this group?** The most obvious answer is the teacher, although some could suggest higher "levels" of authority such as the Sunday school superintendent, the youth pastor or senior pastor, the Bible, and so forth.
- **Once you leave this classroom, who is your next immediate authority?** Answers could include parents, the senior pastor, the students themselves, and so forth.
- **When you are driving a car, who is your authority?** Answers could include the police, the government, parents, the driving instructor, and so forth.
- **When you are at school, who is your authority?** Answers could include the teacher, the principal, and so forth. **Who is your authority in the workplace?** Answers could include the supervisor, the company owner, the secretary, and so forth.
- **Who is always your authority?** Students may acknowledge God or Jesus, and some may recognize their parents as the ultimate authority no matter where they are.

When you are ready to move on, say, **We each have many authorities in our lives. Let's see how respecting and being obedient to those authorities is pleasing to God.**

STRAIGHT AWAY

Leading through the Session

Explore the Bible passage.

Read together 1 Thessalonians 4:1–12 and discuss the following questions:
- **What is sanctification? What does it mean to be sanctified?** Sanctification is to be made holy or without sin. To be sanctified is to be set apart for God's holy purposes.
- **See Romans 9:20–21 and 2 Timothy 2:20–22. How do these passages bring clarity to the source of sanctification?** Accept reasonable answers and talk with the students about the truth that God (not we) does the

sanctifying. Our participation is definitely required, but without the work of God we cannot live holy lives.

- **Just what role do we play in the process of our own sanctification?** Paul advised that we stay away from sexual immorality, love our brothers and sisters, refrain from lust, and so forth. All of these answers focus on our being obedient to the authority of Jesus in our lives. Point out that if we push the boundaries in these areas, we are likely to get burned.
- **Why is self-control such a difficult practice, especially in the realm of our sexuality?** This may be a sensitive topic for some of your students. Encourage their respectful and honest feedback on this topic. Self-control is very difficult in areas where we are battling against natural desires and selfishness. Hormones are very powerful and have a purpose, but they can also get us into trouble. We also have to deal with curiosity; peer pressure; negative input from movies, television, magazines, and the media; lower expectations from adults and authorities (i.e., "Teens are going to be sexually active anyway!"); and so forth.
- **This passage makes reference to God's punishment for those who sin in such matters. What do you think that punishment can look like?** Allow the students to express their opinions on this question. All actions—good and bad—have consequences in this life—good and bad. The Bible also indicates a coming judgment by God for all people, calling us into account for the lives we have lived.
- **How can we be successful in overcoming the strong desires within us and our tendencies toward sinning in these ways?** Again, allow the students to make suggestions about using their own will to overcome these temptations in many different and creative ways: look away before three seconds pass from those of the opposite gender who attract us; avoid movies and television shows that we know could cause us to stumble; listen to music that supports godly morals; and so forth. Paul pointed out that the Holy Spirit is given to us as a gift from God to help us in these matters.
- **Why did Paul say that he did not need to write to the Thessalonians about love—and then go ahead and write about it anyway?** Paul recognized that whether or not we are doing well at something there is always room for improvement. Reminders of things we already know are always helpful as they focus us back in on what it is that we need to do. Paul was aware that loving one another is a part of an active faith that pleases God.
- **Why do you think Paul wanted the Thessalonians to win the respect of outsiders? Shouldn't they just have focused on pleasing God? Do we also need to have the respect of outsiders? Why or why not?** Paul wanted the Thessalonians to be aware that in their lives and actions they were called to be ambassadors for Christ and the Christian faith. This is a calling that all believers have in life. We are invited to be the hands and feet of God through our actions and the interactions that we have with people outside the faith every day. If people respect us, this can move them closer to a respect of their heavenly Father as they see the effect God has had on our lives.

Say, **Paul knew that as his friends lived in obedience to the will of God, their lives would be pleasing to God.**

THE TURN

Make a list.

Invite the students to focus in again on 1 Thessalonians 4:1–12. Encourage them to identify the ways Paul listed that we can do God's will. As ideas are given, write them on the board. Answers might include being sanctified, avoiding sexual immorality, learning to control our own bodies, not doing wrong or taking advantage of others, loving one another, leading a quiet life, minding our own business, working with our hands, winning the respect of outsiders, and gaining independence. Take time to discuss each of these concepts, making sure that the students understand the term *sanctified* (made holy). Draw their attention to the importance of sexual purity, a very pertinent issue within our culture and even more so in the youth culture. Point out that the rejection of this instruction is identified as equivalent to the rejection of God. Also draw special attention to Paul's idea that even our work is something that can please God.

Say, **This is a great passage for giving clear and concise instruction on some ways that we can please God.**

Leading beyond the Session

HOME STRETCH

Option 1 (Younger Youth)
Listen to "Shine."

Share with your class an audio version of the Newsboys' song "Shine" (from their album *Going Public* and the *Shine Hits* compilation). If possible, bring copies of the lyrics to share as well. After listening to the song, go back through the lyrics as a class and ask, **What is the main point that this song is trying to make?** Invite the students to respond, but be sure to focus on the fact that as we allow God to change our lives, others will notice and God will be glorified by these changes in our lives.

When you are ready to move on, say, **The story of a changed life is the most powerful testimony we can give about the love and grace of God.**

. . . .

Option 2 (Older Youth)
Mind your own business.

Distribute copies of "Mind Your Own Business" (Reproducible 1) or show it as a projection, go over the instructions, and allow time to complete the handout. After a few minutes, bring everyone back together and discuss how they responded to each scenario. Point out that there is not always an easy answer as to whether or not we should get involved in a situation. Sometimes we may feel that we do need to get involved, but we are unsure how to do so. It is very important for us to be attentive and prayerful as we face challenging interactions in our relationships.

When you are ready to move on, say, **If God opens a door to a sticky situation in your life, he will also provide the guidance and discernment for you to navigate the tough waters.**

Note:
Many of the issues on this handout are purposely designed so that they could be answered either way in order to promote discussion. The Bible instructs us that, where legally required and not in conflict with God's law, we should obey the laws of the land; that when we have a question about another person's behavior we should go directly to that person; and that we are to help the oppressed and needy.

Option 1 (Little Prep)
Rate your work ethic.

Distribute copies of "Rate Your Work Ethic" (Reproducible 2), go over the instructions, and allow time for the students to complete the handout. After a few minutes, bring everyone back together and discuss their responses. Be open in sharing about your own struggles with motivation and how God has helped you.

Close the session by praying for each member of your class, asking that God would help each to bring God glory in every area of his or her life.

FINISH LINE

Option 2 (More Prep)
Create symbols.

Bring to class craft items such as markers, colored paper, toothpicks, glue, playdough, cardboard, rubber bands, nails, small shapes of wood, scissors, drinking straws, tacks, paper clips, and so forth. Allow time for your students to each create a symbol to remind them of a portion of today's lesson that stood out to them. Invite those who are willing to share about what they created and what it represents.

Close the session by praying for each member of your class, asking that God would help them to bring him glory in every area of their lives.

Note:
Don't forget to distribute copies of the Portable Sanctuary to students before they leave.

NOTES

REPRODUCIBLE 1

Mind Your Own Business

Read over the scenarios below. For each, decide whether it would be better to mind your own business or try to help. Write either *MYOB* (mind your own business) or *HELP* depending on what you would do.

Your co-worker is not doing his or her share of work and you feel that you are pulling more than your share of the work load. _____

You are walking down the road and you witness a car accident. _____

You look down the hall at school and see your friend's boyfriend hugging another girl. _____

You are in a convenience store with your friend when you notice her slip a pack of gum into her pants pocket. _____

You are sitting on a bench in the park when you notice two children playing in the sand. The larger of the two shoves the other to the ground and begins to kick sand into the kid's face. _____

You think your brother has been spending way too much time playing video games lately and your parents aren't even doing anything about it. _____

You glance in a classroom as you walk down the hall at school and notice your homeroom teacher in there crying all by herself. _____

You are downtown one evening when you notice your pastor walk into a bar. _____

A friend of yours is continuing to do something you advised against. _____

You want to know whom your friend voted for as class president. _____

You think your mom may have lied to your dad about the cost of her latest purchase while she was shopping with you. _____

REPRODUCIBLE 2

Rate Your Work Ethic

Using the scale below, rate yourself on how hard a worker you are in the different areas of your life. A diamond represents the hardest worker possible, while a milkshake represents little or no effort at all. Put a **J** next to the scale to rate your work ethic on your job, a **C** to rate your work ethic in your chores, an **S** to rate your work ethic at school, and a **V** to rate your work ethic in any areas where you volunteer.

Diamond (hardest)

Iron or Steel

Rock

Wood

Rubber

Carrot

Apple

Banana

Jell-O

Milkshake (softest)

Do you really do your best at being a hard worker? _____

Is there room for improvement in any or all of these areas? _____

Do you mostly just "eat" or actually work? _____

Portable Sanctuary

Day 1
Surprise!

A number of years ago our youth group went on a missions trip. The missionaries who hosted us were amazing and generous in the many gifts and experiences they had lined up for us. We were constantly surprised that they were able to treat us so well even though they did not have very much money. After a week with them, we as a team had put together a package of gifts for them as well. One of the most enjoyable parts of our experience there was watching them open and accept joyfully the things we had gathered for them.

Questions and Suggestions

- Read Acts 18:24–28. Do you often find yourself trying to bring pleasure to others by encouraging them or blessing them in various ways? Have you ever been surprised when you were trying to do that for others and they turned the tables and did it for you?
- Thank God for the opportunities he has given you to be an encouragement to others. Ask that this week God would allow you to bless someone in a unique way.

Day 2
Navigation

This past summer I went on a trip to visit my parents in Michigan. While we were there, we drove to Virginia to visit my brother as well. My parents had recently began using one of those little portable GPS systems. Over the course of our travels I became very familiar with the word *recalculating*. I am so glad that I can count on not hearing these words from my heavenly Father who always knows exactly where the destination is and how to get there.

NOTES

- Read Psalm 16:7–11. Have you ever felt as though you were abandoned or lost in the business and confusion of life?
- Thank God for his willingness to make known to you the path of life. Ask God to continue to make you aware and remind you of his presence in your life.

Day 3
Glub, Glub, Glub

One time when I was swimming in the ocean, I had a very intimidating and scary experience. I was body surfing and enjoying the waves when an undercurrent grabbed my legs, flipped me over, and spun me around. I was under the water without even knowing which way was up. I am a relatively strong swimmer, and I have not very often felt that helpless in the water. When I finally came up to the surface, I breathed a huge sigh of relief and thanked God for his protection and preservation.

Questions and Suggestions

- Read Psalm 32:6–11. Have you had times in your life when you felt afraid and unable to help yourself? What is a good response in times such as these?
- Say a prayer thanking God for his protection and for keeping watch over you today. Ask God to help you to trust in him more and more.

Day 4
Control

I have a friend who is heavily involved in sports and fitness. He wakes up early every morning and begins his day with an intense workout before he does anything else. I went out to lunch with him recently. I ordered a bacon double cheeseburger, a side of fries, and a soda. My friend ordered a junior hamburger and a side salad. I told him that if I had begun my day with a workout as he did, I probably would have super-sized my lunch order since I would have been so hungry. My friend is truly disciplined.

Questions and Suggestions

- Read Proverbs 5:21–23. In what areas of your life would you consider yourself a very disciplined person? Are there areas of your life where you know you need to exercise more discipline?
- Ask God to move you toward a more disciplined lifestyle that will draw you closer to him and bring him glory. Ask him to lead you away from the foolishness of those who lack discipline.

Day 5
Payday

During my years of college, I accumulated a large amount of debt in the form of student loans. I am grateful for the education I received and would do it all again in a heartbeat, but my debt did have a great influence on how I spent my money in the years following my graduation. My wife and I made sacrifices in our spending habits in order to pay off those loans. A few years ago we made the final payment. To celebrate, my wife and I bought a new car to share. We have jokingly referred to this car as our "payday" for the years of discipline leading up to paying off our student loans.

Questions and Suggestions

- Read Revelation 22:8–13. Are there times when you feel as though the sacrifices you are making to live a life pleasing to God are a huge burden to carry? What helps you get through those feelings?
- Ask God to give you joy as you serve him out of an attitude of gratitude. Thank God also for the great reward you will someday experience after this life on earth—a life that is often filled with difficulty and challenge.

UNIT TWO
INTRO

Making the Decision

SESSION 1
The Salvation Plan

SESSION 2
The Eternal Plan

SESSION 3
Chosen to Rise Above

SESSION 4
Time to Get Busy!

MAKING THE DECISION

The New Testament epistles are consistent in supporting the plan laid out in the Gospels for our salvation, from the decision to follow Christ to the activity and change of living that comes from that decision.

Session 1 explores our call to acknowledge and accept God's salvation through Jesus Christ. Session 2 examines our call to pray for one another so that God will make us worthy of his call and empower us to fulfill it. Session 3 focuses on our call to persevere in our faith. Session 4 looks at our call as Christians to prayer and hard work.

Be sure your students have the opportunity to make decisions for Christ—and the encouragement to get busy once they have done so.

Unit 2 Special Prep

Session 1—For WARM UP, Option 1 (Little Prep), you can use candy or other small prizes. Option 2 (More Prep) requires guests to visit the class; you can also use candy or other small prizes. FINISH LINE, Option 2 (More Prep), calls for an opportunity to attend or watch a crusade.

Session 2—WARM UP, Option 2 (More Prep), requires some personal, meaningful letters from your own life. FINISH LINE, Option 2 (More Prep), calls for adults from your congregation to serve as prayer partners for your students.

Session 3—WARM UP, Option 2 (More Prep), requires water hoses and a water source, and arrangements for water activities. FINISH LINE, Option 2 (More Prep), calls for a visit to a jail or prison, or a visit from a law enforcement officer.

Session 4—WARM UP, Option 2 (More Prep), requires an opportunity to work (and eat) in a restaurant. STARTING LINE, Option 1 (Younger Youth), calls for a visit from your senior pastor. FINISH LINE, Option 2 (More Prep), requires an opportunity for your group to attend a job fair.

Leading into the Session

Warm Up

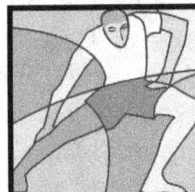

Option 1 Play Two Truths and a Lie.
LITTLE PREP *Candy or other small prizes (optional)*
Option 2 Play Whose Story Is It?
MORE PREP *Guests to visit the class; candy or other small prizes (optional)*

Starting Line

Option 1 Discuss "white lies."
YOUNGER YOUTH
Option 2 Lead a discussion on truth.
OLDER YOUTH

Leading through the Session

Straight Away

Explore the Bible passage.
Bibles

The Turn

Discuss choosing a path.
Reproducible 1, pens or pencils

Leading beyond the Session

Home Stretch

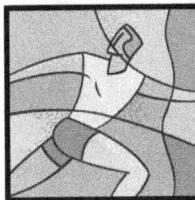

Option 1 Complete a self-assessment.
YOUNGER YOUTH *Reproducible 2, pens or pencils*
Option 2 Compare and contrast.
OLDER YOUTH *Chalkboard or dry erase board*

Finish Line

Option 1 Consider a plan of action.
LITTLE PREP *Paper, pens or pencils*
Option 2 Attend a crusade.
MORE PREP *Opportunity to attend or watch a crusade*

SESSION 1

THE SALVATION PLAN

Bible Passage
1 Thessalonians 4:13—5:11

Key Verse
He died for us so that, whether we are awake or asleep, we may live together with him. —1 Thessalonians 5:10

Main Thought
We are called to acknowledge and accept God's salvation through Jesus Christ.

55

Bible Background

During the period when Paul, Silas, and Timothy stayed in Thessalonica, they worked as evangelists. Part of the work of evangelism included an explanation of the gospel. Part of this would have included the expectation that the end of the age was near, and the Lord would soon return. After the missionaries' departure, the Thessalonian church continued in this expectation.

Paul reminded the Thessalonian believers that the Day of the Lord would come "like a thief in the night" (1 Thess 5:2). Despite speculation about the exact timing, no one on earth could be certain when the end of the age would dawn. The end, in other words, would come suddenly, without warning. To hope in Christ, therefore, is not an excuse for idleness; it is a call to *always* be ready for the Lord's return.

In his writing to the Thessalonians, Paul did not specifically focus his teaching on the kingdom of God. His instruction concerned the end of time. If it is teaching on the Kingdom that one seeks, better to read the Gospels than the letters of the New Testament. It is not at all self-evident that the Kingdom and the end of the age concern the same issues. Jesus teaching on the Kingdom concerns the present reign and ruling activity of God. Jesus' statement that the Kingdom is "among you" (Luke 17:21, NRSV) is phrased in the present tense—the Kingdom is here, and it is also in a certain sense "not yet." But in 1 Thessalonians Paul was speaking of the return of Christ at the end of the age. In the wake of this return, Christians will be caught up to meet the Lord in the air. Christian hope in God is sustained by the vision of eternal friendship with God.

Some final questions remain: What do we do in the meantime? How shall we occupy the time while we wait for the Lord's return? Are we to wait in the manner of an airline passenger, idly whiling away the time while we wait for the boarding call? From Paul's point of view, it is bad Christian practice to sit in idleness. There is work to be done, prompted by our faith. And there is love, God's love, which the world does not understand—and which it is our privilege to offer in imitation of the Christ who will return.

Leading into the Session

Option 1 (Little Prep)
Play Two Truths and a Lie.

Invite each student (or if the class if large, invite three or four volunteers) to think of two statements about themselves that are true and one statement about themselves that is false. Ask them to choose facts that others in the class are not likely to know. Allow the students to take turns sharing their three facts, while the rest of the class members guess which statement is false. If you wish, you can award candy or other small prizes to any students who can stump the class with their false answers.

Say, **Some of us are better than others at hiding the truth or at discerning the truth.**

WARM UP

Note:
If you sent the Portable Sanctuary home with students last week, take some time at the beginning of this session to review and discuss their experience.

Option 2 (More Prep)
Play Whose Story Is It?

Invite three or four guests to visit the class and be panel members for this activity. These should be people whom the students know but do not know very well. Ask your panel members to write a story about something funny or outrageous that happened to them (a true story). Ask them to choose stories that the students would not know.

During class, sit your guests in a row and introduce them by name. Read one of the stories at random, omitting any names that have been included. The students then have three minutes to ask questions of the panel participants. Each participant should answer the questions as if the event actually happened to him or her, even if it did not. Remind the participants beforehand that the manner in which they answer the questions can possibly stump the audience. Their objective is not to be discovered. If the participant answers questions firmly, quickly, and assuredly, the audience will be thrown off track. The audience may not ask the participants directly if it was their story.

After each story has been told and questions asked and answered, reveal what happened to whom. If you wish, you can award candy or other small prizes to any students who correctly match the stories with their authors.

Say, **Some of us are better than others at hiding the truth or at discerning the truth.**

Option 1 (Younger Youth)
Discuss "white lies."

Ask, **What is a "white lie"?** This term refers to a "smaller" lie, a lie that is deemed insignificant, or a "half-truth." Invite your students to give examples of this concept. Here are some possibilities:
- **Q: Did you eat the cookies? A: No, I did not.** (But I took them and gave them to the person who did.)
- **Q: Did you tell her my secret? A: No, I did not.** (But she kept asking me questions, and I answered yes and no until she figured it out.)

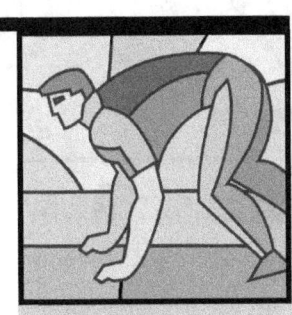

STARTING LINE

57

- Q: Do you like my new dress? A: Yes, I do. (Well, I do if your intent is to wear it to a Halloween party!)

Ask, **What is the danger in lying—even telling "little white lies"?** When we tell one lie, we have to keep telling more and more lies to cover it up, until we lose track of the lies we have already told. When we are caught lying, our credibility is destroyed. Others don't know when they can trust us—if they can at all.

When you are ready to move on, say, **Let's look at some important truths that the Apostle Paul wrote about.**

. . . .

Option 2 (Older Youth)

Lead a discussion on truth.

Utilize any or all of the following questions to generate discussion around the concept of truth:

- **What is "truth"?**
- **What does it mean to believe in something?**
- **How can you tell if something is true or not?** Modern science would tell us that the way to determine whether or not something is true is to "prove it" by subjecting it to rigorous testing.
- **Do you think that there are some things that cannot be scientifically proven?** What are some examples?
- **What does the world offer as "truth"? What does the Bible offer as "truth"?** Some people feel that the truth of the world and the truth of the Bible do not mix. However, point out that the Bible is honest in dealing with the way life works and the unfair things that seem to happen even when we do our best to follow God. Pushing the Bible to be a scientific textbook can lead to some false conclusions. We need the truth of God's Word as a base to provide wisdom and discernment in dealing with the "truths" of this world.

When you are ready to move on, say, **Let's look at some important truths that the Apostle Paul wrote about.**

Leading through the Session

Straight Away

Explore the Bible passage.

Read together 1 Thessalonians 4:13—5:11. Due to the length of this passage, you may wish to have volunteers read different sections, and to stop and discuss each section after it is read. Utilize the following questions:

- **What was Paul encouraging the people from Thessalonica to do?** To gain a new perspective of death based on the truth of Jesus Christ: Those who die in Christ will live again, just as Christ now lives. This is the heart of the hope and joy of the Christian faith.
- **How do people with no hope in eternal life grieve?** They are either resigned to the fact that the end of life on this earth is all there is, or they are distressed at the uncertainty of what may have happened to their loved ones after death. Point out that it's okay to be a little anxious over the unknowns of passing from this life into the next, but we do not need to worry about *where* we are headed.

- **How did Paul depict the coming of the Lord?** As a sudden and unpredictable event, one that we should be ready for, even though we don't know when it will come.
- **What type of life did Paul encourage the believers to live?** A sober or self-controlled life full of faith and love. This refers to being sharp in mind and fully aware of God's expectations.
- **Paul said that those who are awake and those who are asleep may live in Christ. How can that be an encouragement to us?** Being "asleep" is another way of saying "dead." If we die in Christ, then we will live in him. If we are still living this life and follow Christ, then we are living in him. There is no final death for those who believe in Christ. Our loved ones who have died in the faith are with Christ—and so are we.
- **What has happened to every group or individual who has predicted an exact time for the return of Christ?** They have all been proven wrong—100 percent of them! Some people who have made false predictions about the return of Christ continue to preach about this and other things—and people still listen to them! The goal is not to know *when* it will happen—it's to be ready for it whenever it does happen.
- **Why would the people at Thessalonica need to hear Paul's encouragement? Why do we?** There was harsh persecution of Christians at the time Paul wrote this. Even today Christians are severely persecuted in many parts of the world, although we don't usually face that in North America. Whatever troubles we may face in life—whether or not they are the result of persecution for our faith—we can be encouraged by the presence of the Spirit of God in our lives and by the hope and assurance that something better awaits us in eternity.
- **What is the key to our looking forward to the coming of Christ and our hope in his return?** Look again at 1 Thessalonians 5:10. Because we have been saved through Christ, we can look forward to what he has for us in the future. Jesus Christ died for us so that we can live with him forever.

Say, **Paul knew the importance of acknowledging and accepting God's salvation through Jesus Christ.**

The Turn

Discuss choosing a path.

Distribute copies of "Choosing a Path" (Reproducible 1) or show it as a projection. After giving students time to consider the handout, discuss the following questions:

- **What does this picture show?** It shows a person deciding between two paths.
- **What do the paths lead to?** One path leads to eternal reward, and one to eternal punishment.
- **What is the person at the crossroads doing?** The person is trying to decide which way is the "true" way to go.

Invite the students to think of ways to describe the two paths and to write these descriptions on the paths. For example, they might say, "God's way" or "the narrow road" for the way to eternal life, and "own road" or "world's road" for the road to eternal punishment. Point out that the road to salvation is not necessarily an "easy" road in this world. However, we have hope and something to anticipate in the return of Christ. This road is not easy because we endure suffering as God molds us into the people that he wants us to be—people who are more like Christ. Ask, **Because we have this gift of salvation, how did Paul say we should live?** We should be "sober" and prepared, ready for Christ's return. We should live in faith and love and in confidence of our salvation. We should also encourage one another and build one another up as we wait for Christ's return.

Say, **For each of us today, it is important to acknowledge and accept God's salvation through Jesus Christ.**

Leading beyond the Session

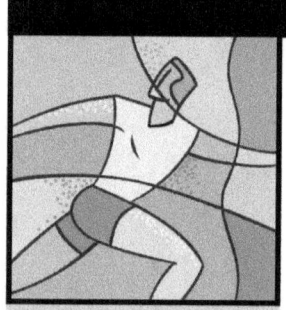

HOME STRETCH

Option 1 (Younger Youth)
Complete a self-assessment.

Distribute copies of "What Will You Do?" (Reproducible 2) and allow for a time of silence. Ask the students to think about where they are in their own spiritual journeys. Are they still at the crossroads, trying to determine what is "true"? Have they already accepted and acknowledged Christ as Lord, or are they walking down the worldly path to destruction? After a time of silent reflection, have them mark with an *X* where they are on this path. Encourage them to be honest in their assessments. Maybe some students have accepted Christ, but they have since rejected him with the way they are living their lives. Next ask the students to indicate where they would *like* to be by marking that spot with an *O*. At the bottom of the paper, the students should write some ideas about how they can move from where they are (*X*) to where they would like to be (*O*).

After a time of reflection, allow the students to share. If the class is large, this can be done in smaller groups. Do not force anyone to share. If the Spirit is leading any students to follow Christ for the first time, refer to "Leading a Teenager to Christ" on page 163 for guidance.

When you are ready to move on, say, **As long as you have breath, it's not too late to choose the path to eternal life.**

· ·

Option 2 (Older Youth)
Compare and contrast.

Make two columns on the board. Title the left column *The TRUTH according to the Bible* and the right one *The TRUTH according to the world*. Ask the students to name Bible truths as you list them in the left-hand column and "worldly" truths as you list them in the right-hand column. After you have a couple of good lists, discuss what you have written. Point out that the world often presents its "truth" in appealing terms and pictures that are impressive but can be unstable. The truth according to the Bible is eternal. It's not always attractive in worldly ways or easy to receive, but it is the right path.

When you are ready to move on, say, **We must have the wisdom and courage to choose the reality of life-giving truth over the glossiness of temporary and shallow truths.**

Option 1 (Little Prep)
Consider a plan of action.

Say, **The time is now—time to choose which path you want to follow.** Remind your students again that believers are called to live with the future in mind—that Christ is returning.

Read aloud the following questions, pausing after each for a time of silent reflection:
- **How can you prepare yourself for Christ's return?**
- **How can you live in faith?**
- **How can you show others love?**
- **How can you encourage others?**
- **How can you show love and respect to your leaders (authority figures)?**
- **How can you care for those who are weak?**
- **How can you try to do good?**
- **What can you do to stay away from evil?**

Close the session in prayer, asking God to help and encourage your students in the process of choosing a path and following in the footsteps of Christ.

Finish Line

Note:
Don't forget to distribute copies of the Portable Sanctuary to students before they leave.

Option 2 (More Prep)
Attend a crusade.

Make arrangements for your students to attend a crusade in your area. Some crusades have youth nights, but attending one of the general sessions is fine. If you cannot attend a crusade, share with your students some video footage from a past crusade. (TBN sometimes plays classic Billy Graham crusades from past decades. The hair and clothing styles are interesting, but your students will see how the power of God moved greatly in those times as thousands of people chose the path to eternal life.) After attending or viewing the crusade, take time to debrief the experience. What seemed to work? What didn't? How did people respond? What did it feel like to see the power of God move and so many people choose eternal life?

Close the session in prayer, asking God to help and encourage your students in the process of choosing a path and following in the footsteps of Christ.

NOTES

Choosing a Path

REPRODUCIBLE 2

What Will You Do?

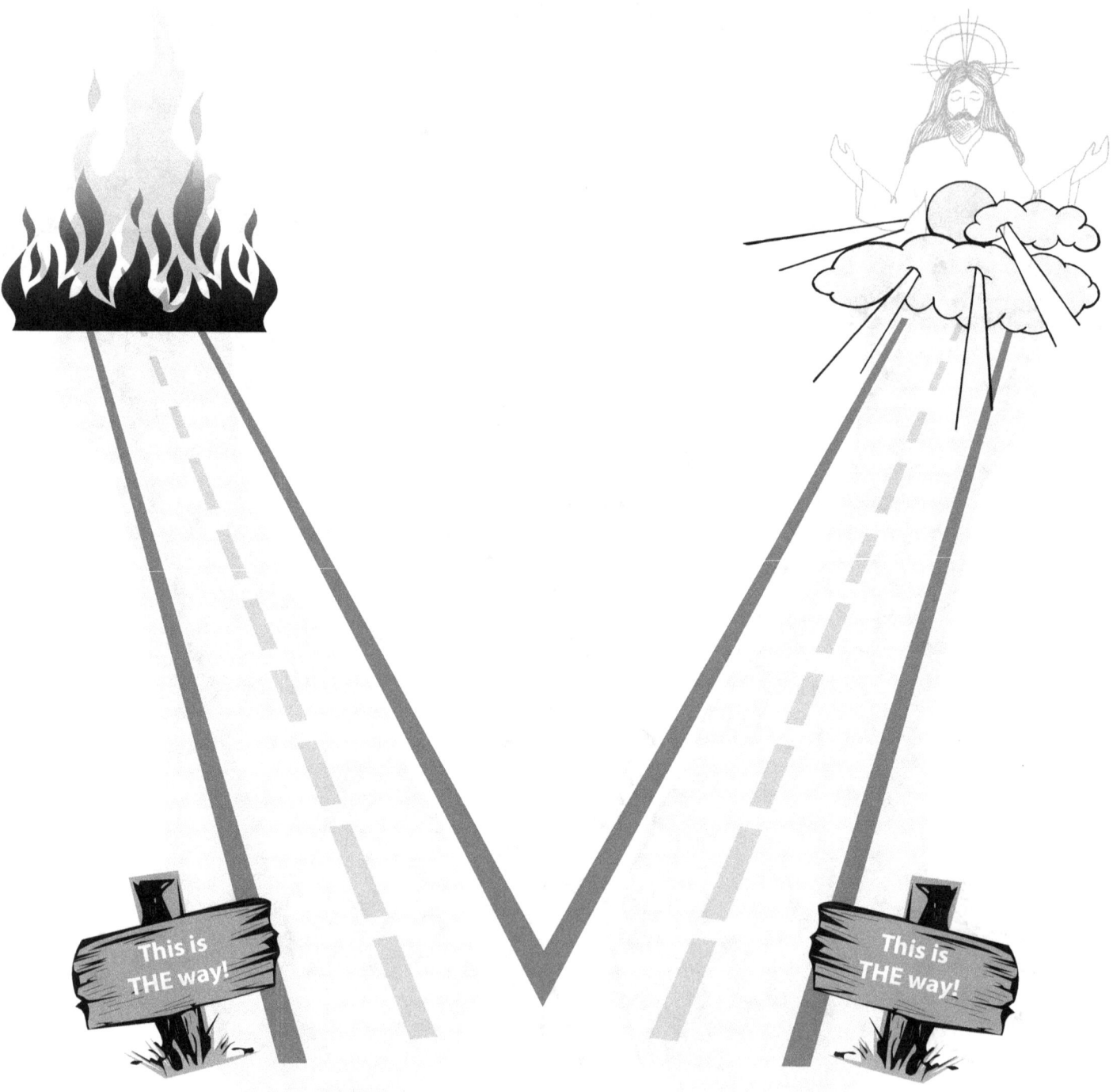

Portable Sanctuary

Day 1
Hope versus No Hope

Hospital chaplains see a lot of people die in the span of a year. Sometimes these people are alone, but there often are family members present. When a family has no hope of their loved one's eternity in Christ, the depth of sorrow is very great. These people wail loud and long and cling to the body of their deceased relative. When a follower of Jesus dies, there is still sorrow, but it's different. There is also a spirit of rejoicing for what the departed person is now experiencing with Christ.

Questions and Suggestions

- Read 1 Thessalonians 4:13–14. Why does the death of a loved one hurt us so much? What will it feel like when Christ returns and death is defeated forever?
- Ask God to make you ready to journey with Jesus when he returns.

Day 2
Flying High

I have never been a big fan of roller coasters. I think it has to do with an early experience when, as a three-year-old, I rode the Matterhorn Bobsleds at Disneyland. I was terrified of the ride but unable to get off until it was done. I actually went until the age of eighteen before I rode a roller coaster again, and even then I only did it to impress a certain girl who was there. I just don't like the feeling of my stomach rising or dropping as I fly through the air.

NOTES

Questions and Suggestions

- Read 1 Thessalonians 4:15-18. What do you think it will feel like to be "caught up ... in the clouds"?
- This week, look for an opportunity to encourage someone else with the hope we have in being with Jesus forever.

Day 3
When the Thief Comes

One Christmas afternoon, we had finished opening presents and eating together as a family. We were standing around in the living room talking, when all of a sudden we saw my father's pickup truck leave the driveway and take off down the street. Only problem was, my father was in the house! A thief had come—on Christmas of all days—and stolen the truck. If we had any idea that the thief was coming, we could have prevented his actions.

Questions and Suggestions

- Read 1 Thessalonians 5:1-3. When have you been surprised by someone or something in a bad way? When have you been surprised in a good way?
- Thank God that when the Lord returns, you do not need to be afraid.

Day 4
Awake and Sober

Why do most people sleep at night? Because the light of day makes it difficult to fall asleep. People who work nights or who live at extreme northern longitudes put dark blinds over the windows so they can sleep when the sun is out. Why might people tend to get drunk at night? Because they work in the day. Night is a time for leisure, and the darkness can hide their foolish drunken behavior. The light of day makes our way clear, and it illumines how we really are.

Questions and Suggestions

- Read 1 Thessalonians 5:4-8. Are you a "morning person" or a "night person"? How can you tell?
- Pray that God will fit you with the spiritual armor necessary to live a sober life of faith and love.

Day 5
Destined for Salvation

What is your destiny? Sometimes public leaders or powerful people share how they felt from a young age that it was their *destiny* to be great someday. This concept of destiny doesn't necessarily have anything to do with God; instead, it usually attributes a person's circumstances to some sort of impersonal force or fate. God has destined you and me to love and serve him and to be saved through faith in Christ. The choice, however, is up to us.

Questions and Suggestions

- Read 1 Thessalonians 5:9-11. How does it feel to escape wrath (punishment for something you have done)? Who took God's wrath on our behalf? How should we respond?
- Again, look for an opportunity today to encourage and build someone else up because of what Christ has done for both of you.

Leading into the Session

Warm Up

Option 1 — Conduct an opinion poll.
LITTLE PREP — *Reproducible 1, pens or pencils*

Option 2 — Share some letters.
MORE PREP — *Personal, meaningful letters from your own life*

Starting Line

Option 1 — Do some boasting.
YOUNGER YOUTH

Option 2 — Discuss the value of prayer.
OLDER YOUTH

Leading through the Session

Straight Away

Explore the Bible passage.
Bibles

The Turn

List biblical ideas about prayer.
Bibles, chalkboard or dry erase board

Leading beyond the Session

Home Stretch

Option 1 — Read about the place of prayer in a
YOUNGER YOUTH — **youth ministry.**
Reproducible 2

Option 2 — Apply your discoveries about prayer.
OLDER YOUTH

Finish Line

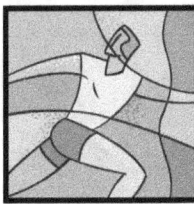

Option 1 — Pray in a different way.
LITTLE PREP

Option 2 — Match your students up with prayer
MORE PREP — **partners.**
Adults from your congregation to serve as prayer partners for your students

SESSION 2

THE ETERNAL PLAN

Bible Passage
2 Thessalonians 1:3–12

Key Verse
We constantly pray for you, that our God may count you worthy of his calling, and that by his power he may fulfill every good purpose of yours and every act prompted by your faith.
—2 Thessalonians 1:11

Main Thought
We should pray for one another so that God will make us worthy of his call and empower us to fulfill it.

Bible Background

The church's situation at Thessalonica appears to have changed for the worse in the interval between 1 and 2 Thessalonians. The first letter is full of warmth and affection for a church that Paul clearly loved and respected. He celebrated the believers' faith, love, and activity on behalf of the gospel. Warm familial words do not appear as frequently in the second letter. Moreover, several of the first letter's concerns are muted or receive no comment in the second.

The issue of eschatology (teaching concerning the "last things," the end of the age) dominates the second letter far beyond the level of discussion in 1 Thessalonians. One explanation for this intensified emphasis is that persecution had become a fact of life at Thessalonica. As the first century wore on, the shadow of persecution lengthened, and the early church found persecution increasingly difficult to avoid.

Persecutions in the Roman Empire came in waves and were conducted regionally. The church in one area of the empire might lead a tranquil life while in another region believers might experience terrible trials. Periods of intense persecution were often followed by long years of peace when pagan Romans left Christians to themselves. It is also the case that official policy was not popular among all pagans; there were those who thought persecution was ineffective and misguided. Before Christians came to the attention of the imperial Roman government, however, they experienced some degree of persecution at the hands of the Jews.

The Book of Acts documents persecution of the first followers of Jesus. Paul himself was among the early Jews most determined to identify and punish Christians. The period of Jewish persecution was most intense until AD 70 when the Romans destroyed Jerusalem and the temple and effectively ended Jewish leadership in the city. In such imperial cities as Thessalonica or any of the other locations of Pauline churches, the minority status of Jews meant that they could not act officially against Christians. Instead, Jewish policy often appears to have been to incite opposition to Christians by portraying them as troublemakers and disturbers of the peace.

Second Thessalonians addresses the increasingly hostile world in which Christians found themselves. The letter describes their situation with apocalyptic clarity: the forces of darkness were arrayed against God, and Christians prayed fervently to God to inaugurate the end of the world through Christ's return. In such circumstances, the virtue of perseverance naturally received heightened apostolic attention.

Leading into the Session

Option 1 (Little Prep)
Conduct an opinion poll.

Distribute to your students copies of "What Do You Think?" (Reproducible 1) and send them out in pairs or small groups to survey people using the questions on the handout. There are some different ways to utilize the survey:
- Students can survey strangers at a nearby shopping center or other public place.
- Students can survey adults at the church.
- You can make arrangements to visit a particular adult Sunday school class and survey the members.

If none of these arrangements is possible, you could conduct the survey on your own during the prior week and share the results.

After the survey has been conducted, bring everyone back together and discuss the results. Identify the questions that had the greatest (and least) number of positive responses, and talk about what these results might mean.

Say, **Most people are at least aware of prayer and many people do pray from time to time, even if they are not associated with a church.**

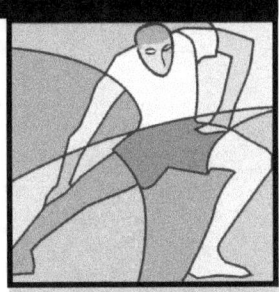

WARM UP

Note:
If you sent the Portable Sanctuary home with students last week, take some time at the beginning of this session to review and discuss their experience.

. . . .

Option 2 (More Prep)
Share some letters.

Bring to class some personal, meaningful letters from your own life. This might include a letter your current spouse wrote to you before you were married, a letter from a family member who was serving in the armed forces, or a letter from a grandparent who is no longer living. Show your students the letters, describe the context, and share the contents. Be sure to explain why these letters meant so much to you (and why they still do).

Say, **Whether a note is written out and dropped in the mail or sent in electronic fashion, it can still be a very meaningful form of communication.**

Option 1 (Younger Youth)
Do some boasting.

Before class, think of some specific ways that you can "boast" about your students as individuals and as a group. The point is not to demonstrate the superiority of your students but to encourage them by letting them know you are proud of them. Some possibilities:
- Send an individual note to the parents of each student. Make copies of these notes and share them with the class.
- Write a short article about specific student accomplishments that might be published in the church newsletter. (For example, *Jared B. was recently honored as MVP on the soccer team at East Side Middle School.*) Share the article with your students.
- Write a letter to your senior pastor or to a youth leader in another church, describing what your group is doing and why you are proud of your students. Share a copy of the letter with your students.

STARTING LINE

69

Ask, **What is the difference between boasting about yourself and boasting about someone else?** Talking about your own accomplishments can turn others off and can be a selfish act. When we boast about someone else, that person can be a little embarrassed, but if the boasting is sincere, it can also be an encouragement to that person.

When you are ready to move on, say, **Let's read about a time when Paul boasted about some of his friends.**

. . . .

Option 2 (Older Youth)
Discuss the value of prayer.

Ask, **What good is prayer, really? Does God hear us? Does God always answer?** Give your students the opportunity to honestly express their opinions. Accept whatever they say without judgment. Be honest about your own experience and struggles with prayer. Point out that throughout the centuries, God's people have sought to learn how to pray more effectively and have struggled to understand the mysteries of prayer.

When you are ready to move on, say, **Let's see how Paul encouraged and supported his friends by praying for them.**

Leading through the Session

Straight Away

Explore the Bible passage.
Read together 2 Thessalonians 1:3–12 and discuss the following questions:
- **Why was Paul so proud of his Thessalonian friends?** Because they were growing in their faith and in love for one another, in spite of the fact that they were suffering persecution and hardships because of their faith.
- **Why is it so important that the people in a church love one another?** This is what God has designed the church community to do. We all make mistakes, and without a deep love for one another, we can be motivated to take revenge or to exact swift punishment. There should be accountability in the church, but love should be the driving force behind it all. It's the quality of our love for one another that draws others to the family of God.
- **How could suffering mean that we are worthy of God's kingdom?** God never promised that serving him would be without trouble. This passage talks about suffering that is a direct result of serving God. But God wins in the end! Our service to him will be rewarded.
- **How does God "pay back" those who trouble his people?** There are certainly consequences in this life to our actions, but the sense here is, again, that there is a future time when God will settle the score and set things right. Revenge is not up to us; we can trust God to do what is right and to take care of it all.
- **Do verses 8 and 9 sound like a description of hell? Why or why not?** The concept of flames in hell comes largely from Jesus' parable of Lazarus and the rich man (Luke 16:19–31) and is supported by some passages from the Book of Revelation. This passage in Thessalonians emphasizes the possibility

of everlasting destruction and separation from the presence of God—not a good thing for anyone.

- **How will we "marvel" at Christ when he returns (v 10)?** To marvel at something means to be totally amazed by it. Since Christ returned to heaven, generations people have worshiped him and served him without seeing him. We know what the biblical record says and what we have experienced personally, but this is only the tip of the iceberg! We will be truly overwhelmed with awe to finally meet Jesus face-to-face.
- **What does it mean to have a purpose fulfilled? What are some examples of a purpose going unfulfilled?** A fulfilled purpose means that something does what it was designed to do in the first place. If a fire sprinkler system doesn't fulfill its purpose, the building burns down. If a class in school doesn't fulfill its purpose, the students don't learn what they should. God has a purpose for each of us. He has designed us to know him, love him, and serve him. To do any less is to fail to fulfill the purpose of our lives—the very thing we were designed for.
- **Does constant prayer mean that we quit our jobs or join a desert monastery so that we can pray 24/7?** No; it does mean that we pray frequently. Closing our eyes while praying at church or when praying at home is a good way to focus, but we can talk to God from the heart when we are driving or listening to someone speak, or at any other time when our eyes are open. This kind of constant prayer conversation with God is a good habit to develop.

Say, **Paul prayed for his friends that God would fulfill his purpose in their lives.**

The Turn

List biblical ideas about prayer.

Invite the students to read through 2 Thessalonians 1:3–12 again and to call out all of the points Paul made about prayer as you write them on the board. Be sure to identify the following ideas:

- *We should thank God for our Christian friends (v 3).*
- *We should constantly pray for our friends (v 11).*
- *We should pray that God will regard our friends as worthy (v 11).*
- *We should pray that God will fulfill every good purpose in our friends (v 11).*
- *We should pray that God will fulfill every faithful action of our friends (v 11).*
- *The purpose of our prayers is that Jesus will be glorified (v 12).*

Take time to emphasize each of these concepts of prayer. Do we do these? How could we do them more effectively? How would it feel to know that someone was praying for us in these ways? How would it make others feel to know that *we* were praying for them in these ways?

Say, **We should each pray for our friends that God would fulfill his purpose in their lives.**

Leading beyond the Session

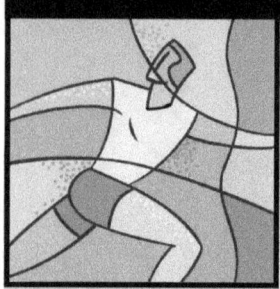

HOME STRETCH

Option 1 (Younger Youth)
Read about the place of prayer in a youth ministry.

Distribute copies of "Prayer Makes It Work" (Reproducible 2) or show it as a projection. Take time to review the handout and to talk about the role of prayer in your local youth ministry. Discuss also the importance of prayer in all of life, not just the limited scope of one youth ministry. Talk about how our prayer life changes as we get older and go through different experiences in life—highs and lows, births, graduations, marriages, divorces, deaths of loved ones, and so forth. Touch on how people are drawn to different kinds of prayer (some pray better alone, some feel the need to pray in small groups to be most effective, and so forth).

When you are ready to move on, say, **Prayer sustains this youth ministry and this church—and it should sustain all that we do.**

· ·

Option 2 (Older Youth)
Apply your discoveries about prayer.

Say, **Let's review just a little. We've seen some of what the Bible says about prayer. So, what good is prayer, really? In light of our discussion, how would you answer this question?** Invite the students to respond. Point out that we have all benefited from the prayers of others. Ask the students to identify specific times when someone prayed for them, and times when they have prayed for someone else. Challenge your students to identify some of the blessings we receive when we pray for others.

When you are ready to move on, say, **If we go home today with some new ideas about prayer and a commitment to implement those ideas, then this session has succeeded.**

FINISH LINE

Option 1 (Little Prep)
Pray in a different way.

Close the session by taking prayer requests. Then invite your students to pray for these needs in a way that is different from the way they usually would pray. Here are some possibilities:
- Pray aloud, even as others are also doing so.
- Kneel at a chair or an altar to pray.
- Lie prostrate on the ground.
- Stand with hands lifted.

As your students depart, remind them to continue to pray for these needs throughout the week.

Option 2 (More Prep)
Match your students up with prayer partners.

Make arrangements with trusted adults from your congregation to serve as prayer partners for your students. Men should pray with boys, and women with girls. You can invite these adults to join you at the end of class to pray with the students or to set up another time to do so. (If they meet at another time, be sure to set boundaries about meeting in a public place, notifying the student's parents, and so forth.) The initial commitment should be for this one prayer experience, but if it works well and the participants are willing, they may want to continue to meet regularly for prayer. You can strongly encourage the students to maintain a relationship with their prayer partners, but do not force them to do so.

> *Note:*
> Don't forget to distribute copies of the Portable Sanctuary to students before they leave.

NOTES

REPRODUCIBLE 1

What Do You Think?

Ask the questions below to different people and tally the results. Use vertical marks for your totals so that you can easily add to them. (For example, 4 would be written as IIII.) Be sure to introduce yourself and explain what you are doing. (For example, "My name is Jared and I am doing a prayer survey with my youth group. May I ask you a few questions?")

YES	NO	
____	____	1. I pray with other members of my family.
____	____	2. I wish my family had prayed more when I was young.
____	____	3. I believe that God hears and answers prayer.
____	____	4. I believe that God hears my prayers but does not always answer them the way I would like.
____	____	5. I have a set time and place for prayer each day.
____	____	6. I wish I knew more about prayer.
____	____	7. I feel closer to God when I pray.
____	____	8. I pray for others who are ill.
____	____	9. I believe I should pray more than I do.
____	____	10. When I pray, sometimes what changes is me—more than the person or need I am praying for.

REPRODUCIBLE 2

Prayer Makes It Work

The Logos System is a discipleship program for all ages that is used in many churches, including in youth groups. This program is founded on the belief that prayer is central to all effective ministry. This is what their staff manual says about calling adult leaders to serve in the youth ministry:

1. Make a list of names of people who love God, love teenagers, and are open to sharing their gifts with others.

2. Pray over the list and write down your thoughts about each person.

3. Take a break from the process for a while.

4. Come back to your list, read through your notes, and pray over the names again.

5. Ask God to give you a sense of whether or not each person would be right for the job.

Before any adult is even asked to consider serving in the youth ministry, his or her name is prayed over multiple times. This gives an indication of the importance of prayer in just one youth program. Think about how important prayer is in the whole scheme of things!

(The Logos System Associates: Church Resource Administration Manual, 1994, 29.)

Portable Sanctuary

Day 1
A Growing Faith

Nothing makes your youth leader happier than to see you growing in your faith. Most of us learn early on how to give "Sunday school answers"—that is, how to say things in Sunday school and youth group that reflect what the Bible says. However, do we really mean what we are saying? Are we actually living those things out with our lives? Someone once said that some people are close to God and some are far away, but it's not the closeness that counts—it's whether we are *moving* closer to God or away from him.

Questions and Suggestions

- Read 2 Thessalonians 1:3–4. How often do you think your youth leader thanks God for you? Ask him or her about it.
- Look around you for how others are growing in the Lord, and give God praise for their growth.

Day 2
Hard Evidence

Courtroom trials are based on a foundation of evidence. What do the facts say? Is the truth clear? Can we tell beyond a shadow of a doubt what really happened? When we look at the evidence, what does it really mean? What is it telling us? There is a rhetorical question sometimes asked of Christians: If you were put on trial for your faith, would there be enough evidence to convict you? God knows the facts, and he will judge what is right.

NOTES

Day 3
Payback!

Grudges can consume us. When some people are wronged, they do not rest until they get revenge—even if it takes years to do so. If they are never able to settle the score, then they never rest. But what if the person who hurt you moves away to where you cannot be in contact? What if this person dies? An obsession with revenge makes some people throw their lives away. But life is too short and too precious to do that. Let God worry about administering justice.

Questions and Suggestions
- Read 2 Thessalonians 1:6–8. What will the return of Christ feel like for those who love him? What will it feel like for those who have rejected him?
- Whenever you're discouraged in life, hang on! God will bring you relief from your troubles.

Day 4
The Heartache of Separation

Those who put their faith in Christ know that death is not the final word. Death was defeated on the cross. The thing that still hurts about death is the separation. We will be united in the Lord again someday, but for those who remain here on earth, there is a time of waiting. We can't hold our loved ones or converse with them. But if they are with the Lord and the Lord is with us, then we are still together. The separation will one day be replaced with a joyful, eternal reunion.

Questions and Suggestions
- Read 2 Thessalonians 1:5. How about *your* life? Is there enough evidence to unmistakably identify you as a Christian? Why or why not?
- If you suffer for Christ, thank God that he has counted you worthy of his Kingdom.

Day 5
Constant Prayer

Obviously, we should not close our eyes to pray while we are driving a car! But driving alone is really a great time to pray. My commute to work is about thirty minutes. My time at home preparing for work is hectic and noisy, but once I'm in the car, I have plenty of uninterrupted quiet time. I have made it a habit to leave the radio off as I drive and speak to God. Even throughout the day, if a need comes to mind, I mention it to God, and if something good happens, I give God praise for it.

Questions and Suggestions
- Read 2 Thessalonians 1:9–10. Who are you most looking forward to seeing again in heaven? What do you think it will be like to finally see Christ face-to-face?
- Ask God to give you opportunities to share your testimony, so that others may someday marvel at the presence of the Lord.

Questions and Suggestions
- Read 2 Thessalonians 1:11–12. Who is faithful to constantly pray for you? Do you consistently pray for anyone? If not, how can you make this a habit?
- Pray that God will fulfill his good purposes in your life and be glorified in all that you say and do.

Leading into the Session

Warm Up

Option 1 Participate in a chair activity.
LITTLE PREP *Chair*
Option 2 Practice standing firm.
MORE PREP *Water hoses and a water source; arrangements for water activities*

Starting Line

Option 1 Compare two situations.
YOUNGER YOUTH
Option 2 Discuss the necessity of repeating tasks.
OLDER YOUTH

Leading through the Session

Straight Away

Explore the Bible passage.
Bibles

The Turn

List principles of perseverance.
Bibles, chalkboard or dry erase board

Leading beyond the Session

Home Stretch

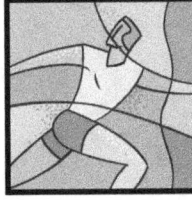

Option 1 Spend time listing goals.
YOUNGER YOUTH *Reproducible 1, pens or pencils*
Option 2 Define words and discuss people of faith.
OLDER YOUTH *Bibles*

Finish Line

Option 1 Complete a faith puzzle.
LITTLE PREP *Reproducible 2, pens or pencils*
Option 2 See the effects of lawlessness.
MORE PREP *Visit to a jail or prison, or a visit from a law enforcement officer*

SESSION 3
CHOSEN TO RISE ABOVE

Bible Passage
2 Thessalonians 2

Key Verse
Stand firm and hold to the teachings we passed on to you, whether by word of mouth or by letter.
—2 Thessalonians 2:15

Main Thought
God calls us to persevere in our faith.

Bible Background

One of the challenges faced by the believers in Thessalonica was the threat and actual experience of persecution. Factors and forces outside the church, which included the Roman government and others opposed to the spread of the gospel of Jesus Christ, at times harried and bullied those who spread the Good News of Jesus as Savior and Lord.

But the local followers of Christ sometimes also found themselves grappling with challenges from within their fellowship. At times false teachings cropped up that spread confusion and increased tensions among believers. In the early portion of the second chapter of 2 Thessalonians, Paul warned against one of those teachings: that the day of the Lord had already come (2 Thess 2:3). In disputing that claim, Paul pointed to the lawlessness and wickedness that would precede the end of the age.

In today's passage, 2 Thessalonians 2:13–17, we find Paul turning from the subject of evil in the outside world and wrongheaded teachers within the church to one of the apostle's recurring pastoral concerns: the spiritual growth of his readers. He began by giving thanks for God's eternal purpose of extending salvation and eternal relationship to men and women who embraced God's truth, as had the Thessalonians. God's salvation opens believers to the transforming, sanctifying, continuing work of the Holy Spirit (v 13) and makes them partakers in the glory of Jesus Christ (v 14).

In light of both the worldly evil that he described earlier and the glory available through response to God's offer of salvation, Paul called on his readers to "stand firm" (v 15). In particular he called on them to hold to the oral and written teachings (which can also be translated as "traditions") they had received from Paul and other trustworthy Christian teachers.

Paul closed this section with a prayer. Among other things, he asked that God would encourage the "hearts" (v 17) of the Christians in Thessalonica. The heart was seen as the seat of human affections and emotions. It was the heart that would quaver in the midst of severe trial. So that they might not "lose heart," Paul asked that God would keep hope strong and alive in those who were attempting to faithfully follow Christ. For human nature is such that we ultimately cannot stand on our own; we must always look to God for the empowerment and strength to do what he calls us to do.

Leading into the Session

Option 1 (Little Prep)
Participate in a chair activity.

Place a chair in the front of the room. Invite the students one at a time to come forward and sit in the chair. Ask, **Why is it that most of you did not have any problem coming up and sitting in this chair?** Some possible answers might include because the chair is sturdy, because the chair can be seen, and because that is an everyday situation for us in school. Then ask, **Did it take faith for you to sit down in the chair?** Some students might say no, because they knew the chair would hold them, or yes because they thought there might be some sort of trick up your sleeve. Explain that faith is believing even when we do not see. Say, **It is amazing that many people have more faith in sitting in a chair than they do in trusting God our Creator.**

WARM UP

. . . .

Option 2 (More Prep)
Practice standing firm.

Make arrangements to conduct some water activities with your students. You will need warm weather, water hoses, and water sources, and your students will need the appropriate swimsuits and towels. For one of the activities, see which students can stand firm while being blasted with one or more water hoses. (Having them stand in slippery mud will enhance this activity.) Recognize anyone who was able to withstand the onslaught of the water and discuss why they succeeded (probably the larger students or those who had better footing).

Say, **When something is trying to blow us away or knock us down, we need to be prepared to stand firm.**

Note:
If you sent the Portable Sanctuary home with students last week, take some time at the beginning of this session to review and discuss their experience.

Option 1 (Younger Youth)
Complete two situations.

Read for your students a list of pairs of situations. For each pair, ask, **Which of these experiences takes more faith?**

Here are the situations:
- **Sitting down in a chair versus riding on an elevator.**
- **Falling back into someone's arms versus speaking to a stranger.**
- **Asking a potential friend to go to the mall versus asking your parents for money.**
- **Trusting a friend in a hard situation versus trusting God for a miracle.**

Feel free to add other situations you may think of. Point out how much faith we think we need in order to do daily tasks. God is always there to help us in any situation. If we learn how to trust God in the little things, then he will help increase our faith to believe in the miraculous.

When you are ready to move on, say, **Let's see what the Apostle Paul told his friends about their faith in the return of Christ.**

STARTING LINE

Option 2 (Older Youth)
Discuss the necessity of repeating tasks.

Ask the students to name some tasks or skills that must be performed repeatedly before we get them right. Possible answers might include riding a bike, driving a car, or playing the piano. Explain that perseverance means not giving up when the going gets tough. The practice involved in riding a bike and the repetition of getting on the bike and falling off can make you want to give up. Life is kind of like that. When situations are tough and circumstances are hard, we tend to look for a way out.

Next ask the students to name different clichés that have to do with perseverance (e.g., "If at first you don't succeed, try, try again" and "When the going gets tough, the tough get going"). Point out that practice or repletion can lead to valuable skills.

When you are ready to move on, say, **Let's see what the Apostle Paul told his friends about perseverance in their faith.**

Leading through the Session

STRAIGHT AWAY

Explore the Bible passage.

Read together 2 Thessalonians 2:1–17 and discuss the following questions:

- **Why would the original recipients of this letter be so concerned about being "gathered" to Christ?** When Jesus ascended to heaven, he promised to return for his followers in similar fashion (see Acts 1). The believers had no idea how long it would be until this took place, but they anticipated that it would be soon.
- **How can we identify this "man of lawlessness" (v 3) who opposes God?** Many people have pegged individuals throughout history as some sort of "biblical bad guy" foretold by such prophecies. This title has been given to various dictators, to the Pope, and even to U.S. presidents! We don't have to look far today to identify people who oppose God and who encourage others to exalt them or worship them. The point is, God is king—and those who oppose him will be destroyed in the end.
- **In who or what do people place their hope instead of hoping in God? Why would they do this?** There are many things in this world that promise satisfaction and success. The constant "high" of physical stimulation and emotional experiences leave people addicted and craving more. When people are sick or in crisis, they can be open to finding the truth of God. But when things are good again, God is often left behind. (Churches were full in the weeks following 9/11, but their attendance soon returned to normal.)
- **How do we share in the glory of Christ? What kind of glory does Christ have?** Jesus did not live a fancy life. He didn't own a home or business, and he had no wife or children. At the end of his life, he was treated about as cruelly as anyone could be treated. But he rose victoriously and eternally from the grave. We are invited to partake in the glory of eternal life in the presence of God that Christ enjoys.

- **What words and phrases in this passage suggest that we should persevere?** We are told not to be unsettled, not to be deceived, to be encouraged, and to be strengthened. These are real challenges for followers of Christ: that over time we will become unsettled or impatient, that we will be deceived by false teachings, that we will become discouraged in tough times, and that we will grow weak in our commitment.
- **How did Paul suggest that we can persevere?** He advised that we should trust God and encourage one another. This is a powerful combination that can keep us strong and growing in our faith.
- **How is it that we are still able to hold to the teachings of Christ?** These teachings were spread by word of mouth, written down, and then copied and told over and over and over again—for almost 2,000 years now and counting! For most of this time, the copying was done tediously by hand. It is truly a miracle and work of God that his Word has been preserved intact for us to use today.
- **In this passage, what was Paul's specific prayer for the Thessalonians?** That Jesus Christ and God the Father would give them encouragement and hope and strengthen them in their good deeds and words. This is God's desire for each of us, that we would more and more say and do the things that reflect his love and his work in our lives.

Say, **Paul encouraged his Thessalonian friends to persevere in their faith.**

The Turn

List principles of perseverance.
Invite the students to read Philippians 3:12–14 and to call out the principles that Paul stated here for helping us persevere in our faith, as you write these ideas on the board. The two main ideas here are pressing on to take hold of that for which Christ Jesus has taken hold of us and "forgetting what is behind." Take some time to explore each of these concepts in more depth. Be sure to point out that Christ has already fought the necessary fight and claimed us for his own. We can never erase our memories of the past, but we should not allow past events or relationships to distract us from our commitment to Christ.

Say, **A constant theme of the New Testament is how we should do what it takes to press on and persevere in our faith.**

Leading beyond the Session

Option 1 (Younger Youth)
Spend time listing goals.
Distribute copies of "Life Goals" (Reproducible 1), go over the instructions, and allow time for the students to complete the handout. After a few minutes, bring everyone back together and discuss the responses. Point out that goals help us stay on track. If we fail to plan, we plan to fail. Discuss the following questions:
- **What is your plan to grow spiritually?**
- **Are you spending time alone with God each day?**
- **Are you reading God's Word daily and exploring its truth?**

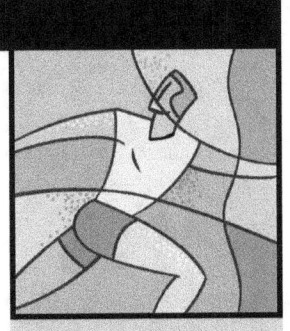

Home Stretch

- Are you spending time in prayer, sharing your life with God and listening to God's voice?

When you are ready to move on, say, **Don't let your commitment to Christ grow cold. Plan to succeed spiritually!**

• •

Option 2 (Older Youth)
Define words and discuss people of faith.

Explain that the biblical concept of *faith* can be well defined from Hebrews 11. Look at this chapter together, focusing especially on verse 1: "Now faith is being sure of what we hope for and certain of what we do not see." The Greek word for faith is *pistis*, which denotes a trusting confidence and belief. Hebrews 11 lists several heroes and heroines of faith from the Word of God. Take time to discuss a few of these names, pointing out that these persons were steadfast in their faith even as they went through difficult times. Invite the students to share about people in their own lives who have persevered in their faith. When you are ready to move on, say, **Life and history are full of inspirational examples of those who have persevered in their faith.**

Finish Line

Option 1 (Little Prep)
Complete a faith puzzle.

Distribute copies of "Faith Puzzle" (Reproducible 2), go over the instructions, and allow time for the students to complete the handout. Correct answers are as follows: (across) 1. patience; 2. logos; 3. mark; 5. traditions; (down) 1. pistis; 2. letter; 4. kenosis; 6. truth.

Explain that maintaining a steadfast faith can give us the determination to pursue all that God has called us to do. It is important to run the Christian race with patience. God will give us the strength to reach our goals. God's Word is truth, and it is never in vain. The Greek word for *vain* or empty is *kenosis*. In other words, God's Word will help us persevere in our faith and it is never empty. It is full of grace and power.

Close the session in prayer. Pray that God will give your students a steadfast faith.

Option 2 (More Prep)
See the effects of lawlessness.

Make arrangements for your students to visit a jail or prison. Age restrictions will probably prohibit you from actually taking your students into prisoner areas, but you may be able to visit the common areas and still get significant impact from the trip. Another option is to arrange for a law enforcement officer to visit your class and speak to the group. The point is to help your students understand more fully the effects of lawlessness and the behavior of those who break the law. How do people fall into such behavior? Why do they do it? How do they suffer because of it? How does society suffer? What hope is there for those who are committed to a lifestyle of lawlessness?

Close the session in prayer. Pray that God will give your students a steadfast faith that stands strong against the temptation to lawlessness and the lawless behavior of others. Be sure to thank and pray for your hosts or your guest speaker.

> *Note:*
> Don't forget to distribute copies of the Portable Sanctuary to students before they leave.

NOTES

REPRODUCIBLE 1

Life Goals

For each area of life listed below, write down your goals for the future—next week, the next few years, and beyond. There is space for you to add other areas.

1. Athletics/Music
_____

2. Friendships
_____

3. Grades
_____

4. (other) _____
_____

5. (other) _____
_____

Spiritual Goals (faith)

1. Reading the Bible
_____

2. Prayer
_____

3. Developing a closer relationship with God
_____

4. (other) _____
_____

5. (other) _____
_____

REPRODUCIBLE 2

Faith Puzzle

Fill in the puzzle by using different parts of today's lesson.

Across
1. We should run the race with _____.
2. The Greek word for *word* is _____.
3. Paul encourages us to press on toward the _____.
5. These are teachings that are practiced because of historical foundations.

Down
1. The Greek word for *faith* is _____.
2. An epistle is a _____.
4. The Greek word for *vain* is _____.
6. This will make you free.

Portable Sanctuary

Day 1
Rumors

With the popularity of the Internet and cell phones, rumors today spread even more quickly than they did in the past. Have you ever received a forwarded post on Facebook or Twitter stating that Starbucks will send you a $10 gift card if you forward the message on to ten more people? Or how about one that talks about a dangerous computer virus sent under the disguise of a Hallmark e-greeting? As they spread, rumors tend to grow and get more and more outrageous.

Questions and Suggestions

- Read 2 Thessalonians 2:1–4. Have you ever heard rumors about the end of the world or the return of the Lord? What do the originators of these rumors do when their ideas turn out to be false?
- When you see people exalting themselves and seeking worldly fame, thank God that you know the truth about who is to be praised and worshiped.

Day 2
Remember

There's a great scene in *Star Trek II: The Wrath of Khan* where Spock has been exposed to lethal radiation and is about to die. But before he dies, he "mind melds" with someone else. This mind meld implants Spock's memories into this other person. In the next film in this series, Spock's dead body has been given new life. When it is reunited with Spock's memories, then the old Spock is back. From time to time we all need a reminder of who we are and what it is that is important to us.

NOTES

Questions and Suggestions

- Read 2 Thessalonians 2:5–8. What lawless rulers are active in our world today? Are you surprised by their actions? Why or why not?
- Pray that God will give you discernment to know what is from God and what is a lie.

Day 3
Refusing the Truth

If you approached a stranger on the street, took him by the shirt collar, and shouted, "Repent or die!" do you think that person would turn to Christ? Probably not. Because of your abbreviated and harsh presentation, this person would likely have no concept of the truth you were speaking. But some people listen to a God-inspired and logical explanation of God's love and God's desire to have a relationship with us. The Spirit is speaking to their hearts—and they still say no. This is a real refusal of the truth.

Questions and Suggestions

- Read 2 Thessalonians 2:9–10. Do you know anyone who is refusing to accept the truth of God? How can you help this person and pray for him or her?
- Ask God to give you a deeper love and understanding of his truth.

Day 4
Powerful Delusions

One description of our need for God is that we all have a "God-shaped hole" in our hearts that only God can fill, and we will never be satisfied until we find God. This is an appropriate description, but what about those people who seem perfectly content without God? The Bible warns us that the lies of the enemy are very convincing and powerful. Some people do not know God and experience a measure of happiness, but they don't know what they're missing.

Questions and Suggestions

- Read 2 Thessalonians 2:11–12. When did you decide to turn to Christ? What was it that convinced you to do so?
- Pray that God will give you opportunities to speak truth to those who are deluded into thinking that their own ways are best.

Day 5
Encouragement from the Lord Himself

Life had never looked so bad. Her parents were breaking up, the bank was taking the house, and her best friend had betrayed her. Even her body seemed to be falling apart, for she was suffering from headaches and lack of energy. She cried out to God. *How can I make it through?* she thought. And then, without warning, the unmistakable and unexplainable peace of God flooded her heart. The tears of gratitude fell. The Lord Jesus Christ himself had given her peace.

Questions and Suggestions

- Read 2 Thessalonians 2:13–16. When have you been in deep despair and felt the peace of Christ calming your heart?
- Today, may our Lord Jesus Christ himself and God our Father, who loved us and by his grace gave us eternal encouragement and good hope, encourage your heart and strengthen you in every good deed and word.

Leading into the Session

Warm Up

Option 1 — Analyze personal spending habits.
LITTLE PREP — *Reproducible 1, pens or pencils*

Option 2 — Work for your food!
MORE PREP — *Opportunity to work (and eat) in a restaurant*

Starting Line

Option 1 — Analyze a pastor's schedule.
YOUNGER YOUTH — *Visit from your senior pastor*

Option 2 — Identify personal attitudes toward work.
OLDER YOUTH — *Reproducible 2, pens or pencils*

Leading through the Session

Straight Away

Explore the Bible passage.
Bibles

The Turn

Provide some context.
Bibles

Leading beyond the Session

Home Stretch

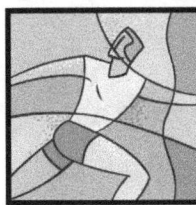

Option 1 — Define what is right.
YOUNGER YOUTH — *Bible, chalkboard or dry erase board*

Option 2 — Discuss money, work, and welfare.
OLDER YOUTH

Finish Line

Option 1 — Discuss work options.
LITTLE PREP

Option 2 — Make work plans.
MORE PREP — *Opportunity to attend a job fair*

SESSION 4

TIME TO GET BUSY!

Bible Passage
2 Thessalonians 3:1–15

Key Verse
Brothers and sisters, do not be weary in doing what is right.
—2 Thessalonians 3:13, NRSV

Main Thought
Christians are called to prayer and hard work.

Bible Background

Today's passage contains a strict warning against idleness. Note that sometimes Paul commanded. Sometimes he pleaded. Sometimes he exhorted. Here Paul commands "in the name of the Lord" (v 6). Such language surely indicates that Paul meant business. Those who were working were to shun those who were not (v 14). What was Paul's problem with idleness?

In the first place, idleness contradicts the Pauline example. He worked to support himself while among the Thessalonians. They could do the same. Paul believed that his example indeed showed the pattern for Christian living on the matter of work. He believed this so strongly that he laid down this rule: "If a man will not work, he shall not eat" (v 10). Second, idleness unfairly burdens those who do work. Christians should not take such advantage of one another. Third, idleness, as the Puritans used to say, is the devil's workshop. Those who are not busy (presumably at work) all too easily become busybodies. Too much time on one's hands leads to meddlesome behavior and, potentially, scandal. No good comes from idleness.

None of this should be taken to mean that Paul thought that Christians should never help one another. Quite the contrary is true! The strong should bear the burdens of the weak. But weakness is one thing, idleness quite another.

A few words must be said about Paul's instruction that Christians are to shun the idle as well as others who do not "live according to the teaching you received from us" (v 6). The intent of shunning is not to inflict punishment on the unrepentant sinner. "Do not," says Paul, "regard him as an enemy" (v 15). The Christians at Thessalonica were not to segregate themselves from the idle in order to keep themselves holy, blameless, and pure. Rather the practice of shunning was intended to be redemptive. Withdrawing from fellowship with the unrepentant was for the purpose of encouraging in them feelings of shame and sadness. By refusing to associate with those who had fallen away, Christians meant to call attention to the seriousness of this condition. Shunning focused on the ultimate reclamation of the disobedient by calling to their attention the gravity of their situation. Paul warned the church that its shunning of the unrepentant should never be vindictive or for the purpose of inflicting punishment. To shun is to warn as we would a beloved member of our own families.

Leading into the Session

Option 1 (Little Prep)
Analyze personal spending habits.

Distribute copies of "Where My Money Goes" (Reproducible 1), go over the instructions, and allow time to complete the handout. Assure the students that their spending information will be private and that they will not be asked to reveal it, but after the worksheets are complete, invite those who are willing (including yourself!) to share as they wish. Now ask your students to go a step further and estimate how much they will spend on each item in a full year. Some people may be amazed at how much they spend on a certain thing in a year's time. There is no need for you to make any remarks or judgments about their sharing; just allow them to share with one another some of their observations on their own use of money.

Say, **At this point in your life, the work of your parents is probably the biggest source of the money that you spend (or that is spent on you).**

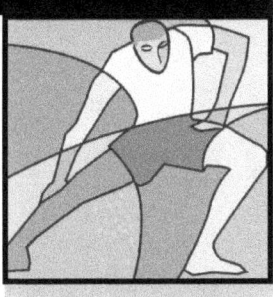

WARM UP

Note:
If you sent the Portable Sanctuary home with students last week, take some time at the beginning of this session to review and discuss their experience.

Option 2 (More Prep)
Work for your food!

Arrange for your students the opportunity to do simple work at a restaurant. This will work best for a small group, and should be fairly easy to set up if someone in your church owns his or her own restaurant. Arrange for the students to wash dishes or bus tables, and then reward them with whatever meal the restaurant owner is willing to furnish in return. Point out that in Bible times, people did not always work for money; oftentimes they were paid in food or in the raw materials needed to build and sustain a household.

Say, **This morning, the work of your hands enabled you to eat.**

Option 1 (Younger Youth)
Analyze a pastor's schedule.

Invite your senior pastor to visit the class and share about his or her schedule in a typical week. Your pastor probably does many things your students are not aware of and may spend more time preparing sermons than your students ever imagined. Be sure to bring out the constant "on-call" nature of a pastor's schedule: when someone dies, is sick, or in crisis—any time of day or night—the pastor is usually expected to respond. In large churches with multiple staff members, this responsibility is usually shared, but for a solo pastor, the constant demand can be quite overwhelming.

When you are ready to move on, say, **Let's see what the Apostle Paul had to say about our work as it relates to our faith.**

STARTING LINE

Note:
Be sure to thank your pastor and to pray for him or her.

Option 2 (Older Youth)
Identify personal attitudes toward work.

Distribute copies of "Attitude Check" (Reproducible 2), go over the instructions, and allow time for the students to complete the handout. After a few minutes, bring the class back together and discuss their responses. Talk honestly about the role of wealth and income in our society, about the pressures to make money and succeed, about the good that money can do, and about the harm the money can cause.

When you are ready to move on, say, **Let's see what the Apostle Paul had to say about our work as it relates to our faith.**

Leading through the Session

Straight Away

Explore the Bible passage.

Read together 2 Thessalonians 3:1–15 and discuss the following questions:

- **How does a person "honor" (or dishonor) the message of God?** Certainly, receiving God's message and acting on it is honoring it. People also honor it when they respect others who follow that message. Our society used to display that respect in giving people Sundays off, in displaying crèches in public places at Christmastime, and in allowing prayers before public events.
- **Why would the word of God be a threat to some people?** Throughout history, power-hungry leaders have felt threatened when their subjects pledged allegiance to God and sought to serve God. Those who passionately pursue God become less interested in feeding the egos of world rulers.
- **How could Paul be sure the Thessalonians were doing the things he had taught them in the Lord?** In a physical sense, he could not. Paul couldn't make a quick weekend trip to see how the Thessalonian church was doing. He couldn't make a call to the pastor there or go online to see what was posted on the church website. Paul had confidence that the Thessalonian church was doing okay because he trusted in the power of God and in the commitment and sincerity of the people there.
- **Why is it good for us to stay away from those who are idle (refusing to work)?** Such habits are contagious and can tend to rub off on us. When we see how nice it is to relax and that it's possible to survive without working (at least for a while), we can lose our motivation.
- **What kind of a work week would Paul and his fellow messengers have had?** Not only did they preach and teach in the church (which would have been multiple times a week and not just on Sundays), but they worked secular jobs in order to earn their food and their board. This would have been more than a forty-hour weekly commitment!
- **Why would anyone in the church (or anyone in general) expect to eat without working?** In an atmosphere of love and giving, we gladly support those who need our help. However, a problem arose in the Thessalonian church: Some people who were fully capable of working were just living off the system. In groups or societies where such support is provided,

some people can grow dependent on it and even come to feel that they are entitled to it.
- **What is the difference between being busy and being a "busybody"?** A busybody has strong opinions and plenty to say. He or she is always busy doing something—but not doing anything that is actually productive. There is an appearance of work, but upon closer inspection, people can see the truth—that this person is just causing trouble instead of doing anything of value.
- **What is the purpose of not associating with someone who has begun rejecting the instruction of the Lord?** It is so this person may feel ashamed for rejecting what he or she knows is right. Paul pointed out that such people should not be treated as enemies; they should be warned in love.

Say, **Paul called the Thessalonians to prayer and hard work.**

The Turn

Provide some context.

Say, **We can understand better what Paul was saying here if we understand more of the historical and cultural situation in first-century Thessalonica.** Share the following points with your students:
- Many, perhaps most, of the Thessalonian Christians believed that the Second Coming of Jesus was about to take place. Because of this, some of them felt that there was no reason to work. Those individuals quit doing all the normal things they used to do; they just sat around every day, waiting for Jesus to return to earth.
- The ancient Jews believed that there was dignity and honor in good, hard work. Paul, a Jewish rabbi, pointed to himself as an example of working for a living. The law prohibited Paul from receiving pay for his rabbinical work; therefore he earned his living by working with his hands.
- There was already a well-known saying that anyone unwilling to work should not eat, and Paul quoted that saying in verse 10. This had nothing whatsoever to do with people who were sick, disabled, or unemployed through no fault of their own. What Paul condemned here was the unwillingness and refusal to work.
- Anyone who rejected Paul's teaching was to be dealt with by the group. Christianity is not a private, individualistic experience; it is a community experience. In this case, those who refused to work were to be corrected by the community of faith.

If time allows, read again through 2 Thessalonians 3:1–15 in light of this additional information.

Say, **Many of the conditions of Thessalonian society are present in our society today. God still desires our hard work.**

Leading beyond the Session

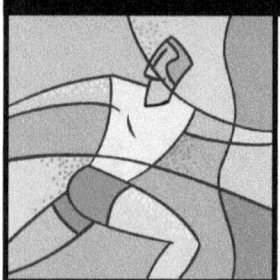

HOME STRETCH

Option 1 (Younger Youth)
Define what is right.

Direct the students' attention to 2 Thessalonians 3:13. Ask them to list all the possible meanings of the phrase "what is right" as you write their ideas on the board. Explain that this verse is often said to mean that we should not grow weary in doing good works. Certainly we should not grow weary in this way, but in this context a more accurate meaning is that we should not grow weary of working. Paul makes the strong point that believers should work and not be idle. Work is "what is right."

When you are ready to move on, say, **Hard work is an important part of growing in God and participating in the community of faith.**

. . . .

Option 2 (Older Youth)
Discuss money, work, and welfare.

Utilize any or all of the following statements to prompt discussion on money, work, and welfare. Be prepared—the discussion may get rather lively!

- **The love of money is the root of all evil. People who work just to earn money are selfish, self-centered, and greedy.**
- **The ability to work for a living is a gift from God.**
- **People on welfare are lazy and should be cut off!**
- **It must be God's will for some people to be on welfare, because Jesus said, "The poor will be with you always."**
- **A Christian is a person who knows how to work. God intended people to work and work hard. This is how we can fulfill our lives and further the kingdom of God.**
- **Sorry, but I can't come to youth tonight. I have to work.**
- **Sorry, I can't work tonight. I have church.**
- **A job is just a way to make money.**
- **A job is a calling from God—how God wants people to serve in the world. And, incidentally, you get paid for it.**

Point out that financial responsibility in our culture is a gradual thing. The older your students get, the more they will work. The more they work, the more money they will earn. And the more money they earn, the more responsibility they will have for their own welfare. Eventually, they will be financially independent of their parents. Right now, they are somewhere between total dependence and total independence. Affirm your students wherever they are in this journey.

When you are ready to move on, say, **God's children are called to work hard, to love one another, and to help one another as needed.**

Option 1 (Little Prep)
Discuss work options.

Talk with your students about practical ways they can begin to increase their income—not just for their own benefit but for the kingdom of God. Fast food jobs are often plenteous, but there may be options that pay better, are more flexible, and offer more opportunity for advancement. Working in a grocery store is one option. Privately-owned local companies can also provide better chances for advancement. If there are individuals in your congregation who own their own businesses, these may be natural connecting points to help your students find employment. Do a little research before class so that you have some strong options to share with your group.

Close the session in prayer.

Finish Line

Option 2 (More Prep)
Make work plans.

Make arrangements to take your students to a local job fair. Even if the students are not old enough or educated enough for the jobs represented, they will get some good ideas about future options. Be sure to debrief the experience afterwards. What new things did the group members learn? What career paths are they considering? What can they do to help ensure their success in this area?

Close the session in prayer.

Note:
Don't forget to distribute copies of the Portable Sanctuary to students before they leave.

NOTES

REPRODUCIBLE 1

Where My Money Goes

In the past week, I spent the following amounts of money on:

$_____ Tithe/giving

$_____ School lunches

$_____ Music (downloads, CDs, and so forth)

$_____ Savings

$_____ Clothes

$_____ Snacks (pop, candy, burgers, and so forth)

$_____ Gifts

$_____ Car (gas, oil, repairs, and so forth)

$_____ Dates

$_____ Hobbies

$_____ Other

Attitude Check

Use the scales and questions below to analyze your attitudes about work.

My job

1	2	3	4	5	6	7	8	9	10
I love it									I hate it

I get more personal enjoyment from

1	2	3	4	5	6	7	8	9	10
Leisure activities									My job

My job interferes with my personal life

1	2	3	4	5	6	7	8	9	10
A lot									Not at all

My job interferes with my church activities

1	2	3	4	5	6	7	8	9	10
A lot									Not at all

Given the chance, I would work

1	2	3	4	5	6	7	8	9	10
A lot more									A lot less

To me personally, Sunday

1	2	3	4	5	6	7	8	9	10
Is special, observed by worship and rest									Is just another day of the week, like any other day

In my opinion, the top three reasons to work are
- ____ To make money; to get ahead in life
- ____ To support myself financially
- ____ To save for my college education
- ____ To keep from being too bored on weekends
- ____ To gain experience in the job market
- ____ To help other people
- ____ To be able to afford a few luxuries
- ____ To serve God
- ____ To keep from feeling useless
- ____ Other: _____

Portable Sanctuary

Day 1

Prayer Request

Churches have many different ways of sharing prayer requests. Many congregations print the requests in the Sunday bulletin or monthly newsletter, while others print them on a separate sheet. Some churches ask for verbal prayer requests during the Sunday worship services, while others have prayer request cards that can be filled out and placed in the offering plate. However the requests are submitted, it's up to the people of the congregation to be faithful to pray for them.

Questions and Suggestions

- Read 2 Thessalonians 3:1–5. How are prayer requests submitted in your church? Do you pray for them throughout the week?
- This week, be sure to get a list of prayer requests from your church, and commit yourself to lifting them each day before the Lord.

Day 2

Watch Out!

I once had a friend who was very committed to serving in the church. In fact, he was the head usher. Every Sunday morning and Sunday night he would be there, passing the plates. At some point, his wife grew tired of attending church, and she became idle. She didn't even come on holidays. Her husband was always on his own whenever he came. Eventually her idleness got to him, and he stopped coming as well. The idleness of someone close to us can spread into our own lives as well, if we're not careful.

NOTES

Questions and Suggestions

- Read 2 Thessalonians 3:6. How important was it to Paul that this command be followed? Why do you think he cared about it so much?
- Take stock of your friendships at church. Ask God to give you close friends who are hard workers for the Lord.

Day 3
Follow Our Example

When those in leadership tell us to do something but do not do the same thing themselves, their words ring empty and betray hypocrisy. I once worked for a guy who expected us all to be precise with our work time. We had to arrive by the minute, never leave early, take lunch at the exact prescribed time, and never conduct any personal business during the day. While he expected us to follow these commands, he spent up to half of his days on personal business, and often ran his personal bills through the company. Not a very good example for his staff!

Questions and Suggestions

- Read 2 Thessalonians 3:7–10. Why did Paul and his fellow preachers continue to work when they could have easily asked for support from the Thessalonian church? How should a church today decide what to pay the pastors?
- Send a note or speak a word of encouragement to your pastors for the hard work they do in the name of God. If they did not work for the church, they could probably be making more than they do!

Day 4
Settle Down and Work!

I know several different families who don't seem to do much work but always have enough to eat. Sometimes I wonder how they make it. Do they have some kind of secret investment strategy that no one else is aware of? Perhaps they had a rich ancestor who left them a sizeable inheritance. Or maybe they just know how to really stretch a dollar! God expects us to do what we are able to support ourselves financially. Charity is there for those who really need it.

Questions and Suggestions

- Read 2 Thessalonians 3:11–13. Why did Paul worry about his friends associating with these "busybodies"? When have you seen busybodies cause trouble in your church or somewhere else?
- Pray that God will give you the strength to continue doing what is right—even when others seem to take advantage of the system.

Day 5
A Brother, Not an Enemy

In the early days of the church, the discipline of the church community was a powerful and effective thing. If you refused to listen and were temporarily cut off from the fellowship, you had no alternatives. Nowadays, most towns have multiple churches. Many towns even have multiple congregations of the same denomination or church affiliation. If people are called to accountability in one place and don't like it, they simply start going to the church down the street, where they are welcomed with open arms.

Questions and Suggestions

- Read 2 Thessalonians 3:14–15. How does your church respond to people who continue to dabble in sin or cause trouble? Why is this such a touchy issue for many people?
- Pray that God will give you the courage to warn those who need to be warned, with the goal of restoring them to fellowship in the church.

UNIT THREE INTRO
The Christian's Focus

Session 1
Advancing the Gospel

Session 2
Living in Humility

Session 3
Looking to the Future

Session 4
Praising God and Getting Along

Session 5
Used to the End

THE CHRISTIAN'S FOCUS

This unit will wrap up our study of what it means to be a Christian by looking at the things that should be the focus of mature followers of Christ.

Session 1 explores our call to spread the gospel even in the face of adversity. Session 2 examines God's call to adjust our attitude from selfishness to humility. Session 3 looks at God's call to adjust our attitude from surrender to perseverance. Session 4 focuses on God's call to adjust our attitude from worry to joy. Session 5 studies God's call to remain faithful to him until the very end.

Our prayer is that the materials in this unit (and in every unit) will be

Unit 3 Special Prep

Session 1—WARM UP, Option 2 (More Prep), requires audio of "The Happy Song" by Delirious and the equipment to play it; you can also furnish lyrics. HOME STRETCH, Option 1 (Younger Youth), calls for four signs prepared before class. Option 2 (Older Youth) requires a guest to share about how he or she shared Christ with someone else. FINISH LINE, Option 2 (More Prep), calls for a computer and data projector, Internet access, and prayer cards.

Session 2—WARM UP, Option 2 (More Prep), calls for objects that can symbolize servanthood. STARTING LINE, Option 1 (Younger Youth), requires saltine crackers or apples. THE TURN calls for poster paper and markers or colored pencils. FINISH LINE, Option 2 (More Prep), requires a guest whose life has gone from selfishness to servanthood.

Session 3—WARM UP, Option 2 (More Prep), requires one or more Mr. Potato Head sets. THE TURN calls for props to symbolize the application of the passage. HOME STRETCH, Option 2 (Older Youth), requires a senior adult to visit the class. FINISH LINE, Option 2 (More Prep), calls for an outdoor area in which to race, and some prizes.

Session 4—WARM UP, Option 2 (More Prep), calls for a large sheet, lipstick, small paper cutouts of eyes and a body, and tape. STARTING LINE, Option 1 (Younger Youth), requires a child's game with different shapes and openings, and confetti (shredded paper). For Option 2 (Older Youth) you can use prepared pictures of famous smiles. THE TURN calls for concordances. HOME STRETCH, Option 1 (Younger Youth), requires magazines with lots of ads. FINISH LINE, Option 2 (More Prep), calls for an opportunity to minister to someone in your church.

Session 5—For WARM UP, Option 1 (Little Prep), you can use a large chain. Option 2 (More Prep) requires a computer with Internet access (either before or during class). HOME STRETCH, Option 1 (Younger Youth), calls for a visit from the individual in your congregation who has taught Sunday school the longest. FINISH LINE, Option 2 (More Prep), requires your group to visit your church's worship service.

Leading into the Session

Warm Up

Option 1 Discuss what makes people happy.
LITTLE PREP *Chalkboard or dry erase board*
Option 2 Listen to a happy song.
MORE PREP *"The Happy Song" by Delirious and the equipment to play it; lyrics (optional)*

Starting Line

Option 1 Share the news.
YOUNGER YOUTH *Reproducible 1*
Option 2 Read "From the Front Lines."
OLDER YOUTH *Reproducible 2, pens or pencils*

Leading through the Session

Straight Away

Explore the Bible passage.
Bibles

The Turn

Discuss how we can follow Paul's example.
Bibles

Leading beyond the Session

Home Stretch

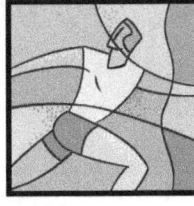

Option 1 Choose a corner.
YOUNGER YOUTH *Four prepared signs*
Option 2 Hear about sharing the gospel.
OLDER YOUTH *Adult to tell how he or she shared Christ*

Finish Line

Option 1 Pray for a friend.
LITTLE PREP
Option 2 Join the 360 Revolution.
MORE PREP *Computer and data projector; Internet access; prayer cards, pens or pencils*

SESSION 1

ADVANCING THE GOSPEL

Bible Passage
Philippians 1:12–29

Key Verse
For to me, to live is Christ and to die is gain.
—Philippians 1:21

Main Thought
We are called to spread the gospel even in the face of adversity.

Bible Background

Philippians is one of a small grouping of letters called the Prison Letters. Paul had been placed under arrest. It's clear that he was in Roman rather than Jewish custody. It is equally clear that Paul believed that he had been imprisoned for Christ's sake and that Christ's gospel would be on trial.

Because Paul had been arrested, he could no longer visit the churches he had founded—including the church at Philippi. His absence gave rise to the question: What consequences might Paul's arrest and impending trial have for the gospel?

Whether in the first or the twenty-first century, imprisonment is an unpleasant experience. Paul would rather have been free. Freedom, however, was not his uppermost concern. Of greatest importance to Paul was that Christ was preached. If captivity served to advance the gospel, then Paul was content to remain in prison.

Paul often found the silver lining of evangelical advance even in the darkest clouds of suffering and obstruction. Here, however, he offered evidence of his feelings. First, even his Roman captors—pagans, remember—felt that Paul had been imprisoned for Jesus' sake. Second, Paul's imprisonment had the effect of encouraging and strengthening the faith of Christians in the district where Paul was a prisoner. Third, the gospel was still spreading.

Paul wrote to reassure the Philippians about the consequences of his imprisonment for both him and them. Because the Romans could be rather indiscriminant about executing prisoners, Paul knew that his death was a real possibility. Nonetheless, he was torn between the possibility of release, which carried with it the opportunity to continue preaching the gospel, and death, which would bring eternal deliverance in Christ.

Recent studies of the Letter to the Philippians describe it as a Christian version of a friendship letter, a common type of communication in the Greco-Roman world. Unlike many of Paul's letters, Philippians does not attempt to settle some problem or confront some issue facing the Christians there. Unlike the Corinthian letters, the tone of Philippians is warm and cordial. In Philippians Paul commended his readers and urged them to go forward in obedience to Christ.

In his letter to the Philippians, Paul took the role of an older spiritual friend encouraging his Christian brothers and sisters to conduct themselves "in a manner worthy of the gospel of Christ" (1:27). As their friend and loving older brother in the Lord, Paul prodded, exhorted, and encouraged the Philippians to grow and mature as disciples of the Lord Jesus.

Leading into the Session

Option 1 (Little Prep)
Discuss what makes people happy.

As the class gathers, ask, **What makes people happy?** Write the students' responses on the board and encourage the group members to speculate further about why these things make some people happy. Responses may include possessions or accomplishments or relationships. Some students may even talk about people's faith making them happy. Next ask, **What makes you happy?** Give the class members some time to personalize the list they have created. Refer to the list and ask, **If any of these things were taken away, would the happiness of people be affected?** The answer would undoubtedly be yes.

Say, **Some people manage to be joyful even in the most difficult of circumstances.**

WARM UP

Note:
If you sent the Portable Sanctuary home with students last week, take some time at the beginning of this session to review and discuss their experience.

Option 2 (More Prep)
Listen to a happy song.

Bring to class a copy of "The Happy Song" by Delirious (from their 1997 album *Cutting Edge*) and the equipment to play it. Ask all of the students to stand and to clear any chairs or other objects out of the way. Turn up the sound system to full blast and play the song. If possible, project the lyrics for the students to see. Encourage the group members to sing along, have some fun, and move around as the song is being played.

After the song is over and everyone is seated again, ask, **What is it that makes you happiest?** Some students may talk about relationships or possessions that they have. Others may talk about their relationship with God. Next ask, **What are the things that make the writer of this song so happy?** This person has found happiness because of what God has done for him in saving his soul.

Say, **Most of us are happy when things are going great. Some people manage to be joyful even in the most difficult of circumstances.**

Option 1 (Younger Youth)
Share the news.

Select two volunteers and give each a copy of "Share the News" (Reproducible 1). Ask the first volunteer to read the first article aloud to the class in as positive and uplifting a manner as possible. The second volunteer should then read the second story aloud in as negative and depressing a manner as possible. Afterwards, ask, **Whose presentation of this article was a better match for the contents of the article?** In both cases, the demeanor of the reader was not consistent with the news being shared. This tends to makes the presentation awkward or even unbelievable. Now ask, **How important is the mood of a person who is telling a story?** The mood can make all the difference in whether or not we really believe what is being shared. Point out that there are many things—including distractions and our own mood—that can affect how clearly we hear the message of someone's story.

STARTING LINE

107

When you are ready to move on, say, **Let's read about the effectiveness of the message the Apostle Paul was preaching.**

. . . .

Option 2 (Older Youth)
Read "From the Front Lines."

Distribute copies of "From the Front Lines" (Reproducible 2) or show it as a projection. Explain to the students that this blog is from a former youth leader at your church who has left to pursue a calling to serve on the mission field. He has set up a monthly blog to update the class on what has been going on with him on the front lines of missions work. After reading the blog, allow the students a few minutes to write or share aloud the comments they might post in response to the blog. Point out that many blogs similar to this exist in real life as a way for missionaries to communicate with their friends. In many cases they need to be anonymous about where they are and the specifics of what they are doing, as they can face punishment from the government or expulsion from the country.

When you are ready to move on, say, **Let's see what the Apostle Paul communicated to his friends about the missions work he was doing.**

Leading through the Session

Straight Away

Explore the Bible passage.

Read together Philippians 1:12–29 and discuss the following questions:
- **Where was Paul when he wrote this letter? What was his frame of mind?** Paul was in prison when he wrote to the Philippians. Even though Paul was imprisoned, he maintained a positive attitude and rejoiced in the fact that God's name was being proclaimed. But there were some signs that Paul was struggling with his situation (see verses 17, 22–23).
- **What were the two major obstacles facing Paul in his efforts to advance the gospel of Christ?** He was in prison—definitely a limiting factor! Also, there were others who were complicating things by preaching out of envy and jealousy and with selfish ambition.
- **What were the two positive results that occurred because of Paul's imprisonment?** All of the prison guards knew that Paul had been put in prison because of his commitment to Christ. In other words, his situation became a witness! The believers were therefore encouraged to speak even more boldly than before. **What was the positive result of those who preached out of envy of Paul?** Regardless of the motives of the preachers, Paul rejoiced that at least the truth of Christ was being shared.
- **How do you see competition between churches today? Do you think that churches compete to have the greatest numbers? the best facilities? the biggest budget? How is it that small churches are often jealous of larger churches?** Encourage the students to discuss these questions for a few minutes. Be sure to point out that ultimately, churches of all sizes need to cooperate together because we have the same mission: reaching those

who are lost for Jesus Christ.
- **What do you think Paul meant when he said in verse 21, "for to me, to live is Christ and to die is gain"? Do you think Paul literally wanted to die? Why or why not?** Paul must have struggled with the knowledge that he was imprisoned and that his life was literally in the balance. Paul was committed to preaching Christ for as long as he lived, yet he knew that his death would bring the reward of being in Christ's eternal presence. He wanted to let the Philippian church know that no matter what happened to him, God would be glorified.
- **How did Paul bring resolution to this dilemma of wanting to remain alive but also wanting to be with the Lord?** He acknowledged his desire to be with the Lord and that that would be better for him, but he also acknowledged that he knew God was not done using him and it would be better for the church if Paul continued encouraging and rejoicing with the body of Christ.
- **What three statements of encouragement did Paul give the believers in verses 27 and 28?** He told them to live "in a manner worthy of the gospel," to "stand firm in one spirit" (stick together), and to not fear those who opposed them. Take time to focus on each of these concepts, what they would have meant in Paul's context, and what they mean for us today.
- **What was Paul's final warning in this passage?** He let his friends know that they also would suffer for Christ.

Say, **Paul acknowledged his own difficulties, but in the midst of it all he rejoiced in the knowledge that the gospel was being advanced.**

The Turn

Discuss how we can follow Paul's example.
Explain to your students how Paul continually faced difficulties during his ministry. He was arrested and beaten. He was shipwrecked, whipped, mocked, and thrown out of towns. But in the midst of all these troubles, there was a consistent pattern in Paul's life. Ask, **What "positive pattern" do you see in Paul's words to his Philippian friends?** Look again at Philippians 1:12–29. Help your students to see the following:

- Paul maintained his trust in God.
- He rejoiced knowing that Christ was being proclaimed.
- He lived a consistent life worthy of his calling.
- He lived and spoke boldly.

Say, **We can follow the same pattern that Paul has set for us as we strive to boldly proclaim the Good News of Jesus Christ.**

Leading beyond the Session

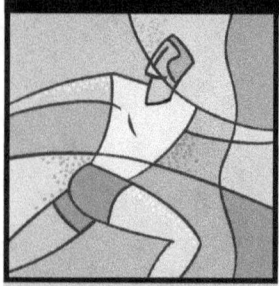

HOME STRETCH

Option 1 (Younger Youth)
Choose a corner.

Prepare a sign reading *A*, another reading *B*, one reading *C*, and one reading *D* and post each of the signs in a different corner or area of the room. Explain to the students that you are going to give them four choices to a few questions. For each question, they are to choose a corner to stand in that coincides with their answer. After the students have made a choice for each question, invite one person from each corner to explain why he or she chose that answer. If there are no students standing in a particular corner, allow one student to explain why he or she didn't choose that particular answer.

Here are the questions; feel free to add your own:

If you shared Christ with your friends at school, what would they do?
- Laugh at you.
- Be polite but do nothing.
- Blow you off.
- Show some interest or ask questions.

Which of the following is the most effective way to share about Jesus?
- Hand out gospel tracts during lunch time.
- Carry a Bible around with you.
- Stick to your morals.
- Pray for your friends when they have problems.

Which of the following is the least effective way to share about Jesus?
- Whenever a teacher asks you a question in class, shout "Jesus!" as the answer.
- Paint a big JC on the side of the gym.
- Listen to Christian music as you walk the hallways.
- Wear a Christian t-shirt that makes fun of another name brand.

When you are ready to move on, say, **There are some good ways and some not so good ways to share about Jesus Christ with our friends.**

. . . .

Note:
Be sure to thank your guest and to pray for him or her.

Option 2 (Older Youth)
Hear about sharing the gospel.

Arrange to have an adult guest visit your class to share about how he or she shared Christ with someone else (perhaps a classmate, co-worker, or friend) who then came to know Christ as Savior. (This activity may be more effective if you bring in a guest rather than share your own story.) Ask your guest to share about some of the fears that he or she experienced and about overcoming those fears. Ask your guest to share about how it felt knowing that God used him or her. Encourage your students to ask their own questions of your guest.

When you are ready to move on, say, **Sharing the gospel can be scary—but it can be one of the most rewarding and important things you ever do.**

Option 1 (Little Prep)
Pray for a friend.

Ask the students to pair up for prayer. In the pairs, they should share with their partner the name of someone whom they would like an opportunity to share Christ with this week. After the names have been shared, the students should pray for one another and then commit to praying for the persons named throughout the following week.

Close by praying for your students, that God would make them bold and effective in spreading the gospel, even in the face of adversity.

Finish Line

Option 2 (More Prep)
Join the 360 Revolution.

The 360 Revolution is a teen-focused evangelism tool to encourage students to pray for their friends to come to know Christ. They choose three friends, pray for those friends six times per week, and seek to miss zero opportunities to share Christ with them. Materials for the 360 Revolution are available at www.chogy.org.

Share with your students the basic idea of the 360 Revolution, using as much of the information as is pertinent to your group and as time allows. Print off the prayer cards, distribute one to each student, and ask the students to fill in the names of their three friends. Close the session by praying for these friends, and be sure to follow up in the coming weeks to celebrate with your students when they have opportunities to share about Christ.

Note:
The 360 Revolution website (www.chogy.org) also includes an evangelism curriculum track that can be used with your students over a series of weeks.

Note:
Don't forget to distribute copies of the Portable Sanctuary to students before they leave.

NOTES

REPRODUCIBLE 1

Share the News

Read the news articles below as your leader instructs you.

Man killed in industrial accident

Few details are available about an industrial accident that claimed the life of a worker at a Springtown concrete plant.

Police officials say Gregory Williams, 35, was killed in an accident at the K and S Materials site on Tuesday afternoon.

Preliminary reports didn't indicate how Williams was killed. A police department spokeswoman said he was pronounced dead at the scene.

The Indiana-based K and S Materials has 220 facilities and employs 8,500 people nationwide.

Jones Institute students donate to help emergency aid services

Students from the Jones Institute recently filled a pickup truck with toys to help the city's emergency aid services.

Students from the school have been raising toy-buying money since March. The toys, which will go to needy children, were valued at over $1,000.

"It's very important to give back to our community," instructor Mary Graham said. "Now we get to see the rewards of our hard work."

The students created gift baskets, made blankets, and sold baked goods to raise the funds.

"These kids did everything themselves," school principal Paul Taylor said. "They wanted to help those in our community who are struggling."

From the Front Lines

From the Front Lines

Greetings from the front lines. This is Tony and I wanted to write and update you as to what has been going on with me. It has been about three months since I left the comforts of home, and let me tell you, I do miss all of you guys. I can't tell you what country I'm currently in because there is so much tension over Christianity here. When I come home, I'll be able to fill you in more on what it's like over here. I really do miss you guys. There are a lot of cold, dark nights where I wish I was back in the safety and security of my own home, but there have been some amazing things that have happened to me here.

Since I have been serving as an English teacher, I have been able to form some great relationships with people in the city. God has really opened the door for me to talk to people about my faith. But that has also been pretty dangerous. The local police even came in to question me about my activities. But even though the government officials have threatened me, the local police officers have been listening to me. I even had the opportunity to pray with one of the officers for his sick daughter.

There are two things that keep me going, even when I want to quit and go home. I know that you guys are praying for me. I also know that God is with me. I'm praying for you guys too. I would love to hear from you.

Blessings and love,
Tony

posted by Tony at 12:22 AM
tags: faith, life, update

Comment:

Portable Sanctuary

Day 1

Paul Establishes the Church

There is always a very unique and special relationship that a founding pastor has with the church that he or she establishes. The church you attend might have a building or a room named after your founding pastor. If you talk to some of the senior citizens in your church, you might learn some stories about your founding pastor, depending on how old your church is. Maybe you are in a new church and know the founding pastor. Paul set up the church in Philippi after he met a woman named Lydia.

Questions and Suggestions

- Read Acts 16:11–40 to learn about the foundations of the church in Philippi. Knowing what you now know about this church, how special do you think it was for them to get a letter from Paul?
- Read Philippians 1:4–11 to find out how Paul felt about the believers in Philippi.

Day 2

Dad

Charles looks up to his dad and respects him more than any other man in the world. Charles's dad provides for his family and loves each of his kids. He spends time with them every day and calls regularly whenever he is working out of town. He has coached Little League teams and helped out with Girl Scout trips for his children. One day as Charles was looking for Christmas decorations in the attic, he found some of his dad's old college papers. One paper was titled "Freedom." In it, Charles's dad wrote about his desire to never have kids or be tied down.

NOTES

Questions and Suggestions

- How would you feel if you were Charles's? Do you think that Charles's dad betrayed his dreams, or were his dreams changed to align with where God led him?
- The Apostle Paul's life turned out much differently than he initially planned. Paul chose to celebrate what God was doing and to strive to serve God where he was, regardless of his situation. Today, ask God to give you joy and to use you wherever you are.

Day 3
Pastor Prakash

In October 2009, Pastor Prakash was attacked by a group of extremists while he was traveling. These men accused the pastor of cheating people. Pastor Prakash leads a small church of eighty people in India and was ministering in a neighboring village when he was attacked. The mob had this pastor arrested and held in custody for an extended period of time. This is not a fictional story. This kind of persecution happens to many Christians, even today. (See the website of the Voice of the Martyrs at www.persecution.com.)

Questions and Suggestions

- Read 2 Corinthians 1:8–11. Do you think Paul ever felt discouraged or down? How did this affect his faith?
- We don't often face the same situations as this Pastor Prakash or as Paul when we share the gospel, but we still have our difficult times where we get discouraged and feel like giving up. Pray that when you are discouraged, God will sustain and protect you.

Day 4
A Worthy Life

Maggie struggles every day with doubts and worries. She loves God and wants to serve God with her whole heart. But she is so afraid of letting God down. What if she messes up and others see her mistakes? What would they think of God? Would that destroy God's name to those she is trying to share his love with? Because of these doubts and worries, Maggie is basically paralyzed. She really does love God, but she is very careful in her efforts to keep it a secret.

Questions and Suggestions

- Read Philippians 1:20, 27. What kinds of thoughts did Paul struggle with here? How did he feel about failing God?
- Paul also gave us some guidelines to live by as we live for God. Read Ephesians 4:1–3 to uncover some specific ways that Paul said we can live a worthy life.

Day 5
When Life Is Comfortable

When life is comfortable, we should willingly take a share of someone else's pain. By doing this, we will tell the world that the gospel is true. What is your first reaction to this concept? What does it mean to you? Have you ever really suffered because of your faith in Christ? Many of us today do not understand what it means to suffer because of Christ. We live comfortable lives, in a nation that has been open to Christianity since the country's earliest days. Perhaps we can help carry the pain of others, and so proclaim the gospel.

Questions and Suggestions

- So, what can you do to take a share of someone else's pain? Maybe there is someone in need of a jacket and you have two. Maybe you can pray for someone from the Voice of the Martyrs website. Maybe you can volunteer time at a shelter or convalescent home.
- Pray that God will lead you to opportunities to share the pain of others—to things bigger than you ever imagined.

Leading into the Session

Warm Up

Option 1 Find words using letters.
LITTLE PREP *Chalkboard or dry erase board, paper, pens or pencils*

Option 2 Conduct a servant scavenger hunt.
MORE PREP *Objects that can symbolize servanthood*

Starting Line

Option 1 Demonstrate the power of speech.
YOUNGER YOUTH *Saltine crackers or apples*

Option 2 Identify hurdles to humility.
OLDER YOUTH *Reproducible 1, pens or pencils*

Leading through the Session

Straight Away

Explore the Bible passage.
Bibles, Reproducible 2, pens or pencils

The Turn

Create a bulletin board or wall display.
Bibles, poster paper, markers or colored pencils

Leading beyond the Session

Home Stretch

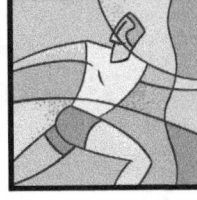

Option 1 Give examples of how to help others humbly.
YOUNGER YOUTH *Chalkboard or dry erase board*

Option 2 Write your own humility poetry.
OLDER YOUTH *Bibles, paper, pens or pencils*

Finish Line

Option 1 Reflect on what it means to be filled with humility.
LITTLE PREP

Option 2 Conduct a servanthood interview.
MORE PREP *Guest whose life has gone from selfishness to servanthood*

SESSION 2

LIVING IN HUMILITY

Bible Passage
Philippians 2:1–13

Key Verse
Your attitude should be the same as that of Christ Jesus.
—Philippians 2:5

Main Thought
God calls us to adjust our attitude from selfishness to humility.

Bible Background

The Macedonians had built a city on the site of Philippi long before the arrival of the Romans; however, after the Roman army destroyed the city, it was resettled as an imperial colony. The new colonists included a number of people who were Roman citizens. Those who carried this designation were a privileged minority in the Empire. The statement "I am a citizen of Rome" constituted something of a boast.

Roman achievement made boasting easy. The Roman army and navy had turned the Mediterranean Sea into a Roman lake, creating the largest empire the ancient world had seen. Roman achievements in law and engineering were unrivaled. Proud of the empire and its achievements, Romans walked with a swagger. Strength, courage, and pride—perhaps even a little arrogance—could easily be listed among the "virtues" that the Romans prized.

As indicated in today's passage, Paul encouraged the Philippians in the Christian virtue of humility. Paul's exhortation to the church in Philippians 2 must be seen as a sharply countercultural statement. Paul understood that living counter-culturally is a natural consequence of following Christ. Humility was not high on any list of Roman virtues. To clarify and strengthen his point, Paul quoted a Christian hymn that pointed to Christ as the model of humility.

For many years, scholars have generally agreed that Philippians 2:6–11 is an early Christian hymn about Christ. It can be broken down into three sections related to the Incarnation: (1) preexistence, (2) existence, and (3) post-existence. The hymn unreservedly states that Christ Jesus is "in very nature God" (v 6). The hymn goes on to say that the one who was equal to God "made himself nothing" (v 7) or, to put it another way, "emptied himself." Verses 9–11 describe Jesus in his exaltation, after the Incarnation. Taken together, these verses constitute one of the most important early statements of Christology—the field of theology concerned with the person and work of Christ.

Some day every knee will bow and every tongue will confess the lordship of Christ. Much like the Romans, our contemporary fascination with power and glory can obscure the manner of Christ's exaltation. If the eternal Son of God could lay aside equality with God, then perhaps humility and unselfish love lie nearer the center of the divine glory than do conventional notions of divine majesty. Perhaps it will be the beauty of holiness and the power of suffering love that will cause us all to drop to our knees.

Leading into the Session

Option 1 (Little Prep)
Find words using letters.

Write the terms *servanthood* and *selfishness* on the board. Distribute paper and pens or pencils to the students and challenge them to use the letters in these words to come up with as many additional words as possible, using each letter in the original words only one time. (They can cross letters off as they use them.) Allow a few minutes to complete this activity, then see who was able to come up with the greatest number of unique words. Spend some time discussing how a person who is a servant gives up her or his rights, wants, and privileges, while someone who is selfish demands these things.

Say, **Our attitude—whether one of servanthood or one of selfishness—dramatically affects how we live our lives.**

WARM UP

Note:
If you sent the Portable Sanctuary home with students last week, take some time at the beginning of this session to review and discuss their experience.

Option 2 (More Prep)
Conduct a servant scavenger hunt.

Before the students arrive, hide several objects around the room that symbolize servanthood. These might include a basin, a towel, a cross, pants with holes worn in the knees, a hammer, a loaf of bread, or a serving platter. Once the class members arrive, ask them to scout the room for objects that can symbolize servanthood. After the objects are found, invite the students to explain how each symbolizes servanthood. If someone picked out an object you didn't hide, that's okay; let the students draw the correlation between the object and how it portrays being a servant.

Say, **Today we will see how serving leads to sacrifice, but selfishness leads to regret.**

Option 1 (Younger Youth)
Demonstrate the power of speech.

Bring to class some saltine crackers or some apples. Divide the group into two teams and ask one team to send a representative to the front of the room. Explain that you will give the speaker a phrase to communicate to the team. For the first round, the phrase must be communicated by speaking through a closed mouth without any hand signals or body language. The remaining students on a team should listen carefully and try to correctly guess what the person is saying. They should keep guessing until they get it right or until you call time. Allow someone from the second team to try another phrase in similar fashion. For the second round, permit the speakers to open their lips while keeping their teeth clenched together. For the third round, the two speakers should say the phrase with their mouths full of saltine crackers or with an apple clenched between their teeth. Explain that how we speak—our attitude and the motivation behind our words—can be an act of selfishness or an act of service.

When you are ready to move on, say, **Let's see what the Apostle Paul said about the influence of our words and our actions.**

STARTING LINE

Option 2 (Older Youth)
Identify hurdles to humility.

Distribute copies of "Hurdles" (Reproducible 1) or show it as a projection, go over the instructions, and allow time to complete the handout. After a few minutes, bring everyone back together and discuss their responses. Praise the creativity of your students in naming these different "hurdles to humility." Here are some possible responses:

Hurdle 1—An "I'm the center of the Universe" attitude
Hurdle 2—A "No one else matters" attitude
Hurdle 3—A "negative mouth" attitude
Hurdle 4—A "We have never done it that way before" attitude
Hurdle 5—A "Don't pin me down" attitude

Explain that each of these hurdles is a common barrier in our attempts to serve others.

When you are ready to move on, say, **Let's see what the Apostle Paul said about staying humble and serving others.**

Leading through the Session

STRAIGHT AWAY

Explore the Bible passage.

Read together Philippians 2:1–13. Distribute copies of "Humility Bible Study" (Reproducible 2) or show it as a projection for the students to use as a study aid. Discuss the following questions:

- **What did Paul say here would make him happy?** Paul said he would be happy if his friends would be unified in thought, in love, in spirit, and in purpose, and if they would be humble and focused on serving others.
- **What are the things that would have motivated the Philippians to have such an attitude?** It would come from their relationship with Christ, the comfort of his love, the presence of his Spirit, and the tenderness and compassion that Christ had given them. When we are in relationship with Christ, it changes our attitude and affects the way we live.
- **What do you notice about verses 5–11?** Be sure all the students can see these verses in print. Verse 5 sets up a poetic passage in verses 6–11. (Point out that biblical poems did not rhyme—even in the original language!) In Bible times, most people did not have copies of the Word of God, and many people could not even read. Certain basic truths about God were sometimes put in poetic form so that they could be more easily memorized and shared verbally among the people.
- **What is so incredible about the attitude of Christ as it's described here?** He was "in very nature God" (v 6)—was, in fact, God—and yet he set that aside to become a man, to come o earth to serve us, and to die for us—a humiliating death on a cross! To Paul, this was the supreme example of a humble attitude.
- **What did Paul mean about everyone bowing to Christ and confessing him? Surely everyone in the world does not do that!** In this life, not everyone chooses to serve God through Christ. But all who die (and we will all do that!) will stand before God. In that day, the events of our lives will

be revealed and everyone will finally see and acknowledge the truth about Christ—even if they have already made the eternal choice not to follow him.

- **What is the difference between obeying someone in his or her presence and doing so in his or her absence?** It's easy to mind our manners when the authorities are watching, but much easier to do our own thing when we know we can get away with it. Paul knew he didn't have anything to worry about; even though he was not there with his friends, he was fully confident that they would maintain their commitment to Christ.
- **What does it mean to "work out your salvation" (v 12)?** Salvation is the free gift of God, but it does require effort on our part. It's more than just a one-time decision; it's a totally new way of life, one that involves a commitment to serving God and serving others.
- **Ultimately, who brings about our salvation?** God is the one who works this in us. It is his will, and there's a good purpose behind what he is doing.

Say, **Paul called his friends to move toward an attitude of total humility.**

The Turn

Create a bulletin board or wall display.

Bring to class some poster paper and markers or colored pencils. Look again at Philippians 2:1–13 and invite the students to work in pairs or groups to make banners that include the text of Philippians 2:5 and illustrations around the words and phrases to help explain the verse. The banners should also be decorated with other images from the Philippians passage, focusing particularly on the poetic language of verses 5–11. After the banners are complete, ask for volunteers to share the meaning of their artwork with the rest of the class. Point out that Jesus was fully God and decided to become fully man to identify with our pains, connect us intimately to God, and suffer for the sins of humankind.

Say, **Jesus set aside his privilege and power as God in order to become a servant and to die for us. Jesus chose this role because he knew it was necessary to bring salvation to all of humankind.**

Note:
If possible, post your students' work somewhere that the rest of the church can see it.

Leading beyond the Session

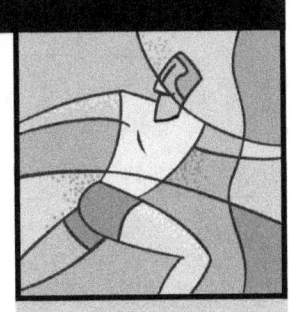

Home Stretch

Option 1 (Younger Youth)

Give examples of how to help others humbly.

Say, **We're going to brainstorm ways to move from selfishness to humility, which involves getting our focus off our own interests. I will give you some different situations in which someone needs help. I want you to give me specific ways that someone could help these individuals.** Share the following situations, pausing after each to write down the students' ideas on the board:

- **A lonely girl at school needs a friend.**
- **An elderly couple in the neighborhood needs their walk and driveway shoveled.**
- **Older kids are picking on a freshman guy.**
- **A homeless man lives in the park near your house.**

- **The parents of a friend at work are going through a messy divorce.**
- **During Sunday school, you notice two young children who live next door to the church playing in their yard.**
- **A poor family needs food.**

After generating some ideas and discussing the situations, point out that we don't have to call attention to ourselves in order to share Jesus Christ with others. When we do something that serves someone in some way, people can observe Jesus' love in action and see him in us.

When you are ready to move on, say, **We can demonstrate God's love instead of just talking about it.**

Option 2 (Older Youth)
Write your own humility poetry.

Distribute paper and pens or pencils and allow time for the students to create their own poems based on the style and content of Philippians 2:1–13. The poems should focus on the love and humility of Christ, on our own call to humility and service, or on some other concept from the passage. After a few minutes, invite those who are willing to share their work with the rest of the group.

When you are ready to move on, say, **Whether or not you consider yourself a poet, God can inspire a deep love and gratitude in your heart for him and a commitment to serve the needs of others.**

FINISH LINE

Option 1 (Little Prep)
Reflect on what it means to be filled with humility.

Ask the students to form a circle with their backs to one another (so they can think with fewer distractions). Ask them to silently consider their responses to the following phrases:
- Humility means to…
- Jesus gave me an example of humility when he…
- I had a chance to show kindness but didn't when…
- One person to whom I need to show kindness is…
- I know that I'm really serving as Christ served when…

Close the session in prayer. Ask God to give you and your group humility in a society that honors selfishness, and pray that your lives will follow Christ's example.

Option 2 (More Prep)
Conduct a servanthood interview.

Invite to your group a guest whose life has gone from selfishness to servanthood. (If you do not know anyone personally, your pastor or youth pastor may have some good ideas.) Invite your guest to share with the class. Utilize the following questions, and feel free to add others:

Note:
Don't forget to distribute copies of the Portable Sanctuary to students before they leave.

- How have your thoughts and feelings about humility and service been changed over time? What happened to cause that change?
- Who comes to your mind when you hear the word humility? What has that person said or done that gives you an image of humility?
- How has the individual you just mentioned influenced you? How has your life changed since knowing the person?

Close the session in prayer. Thank your guest and pray for him or her. Ask God to give you and your group humility in a society that honors selfishness, and pray that your lives will follow Christ's example.

NOTES

REPRODUCIBLE 1

Hurdles

On this page you will find hurdles to humility. In each hurdle write in a short catch phrase to help you remember to avoid these barriers to Christian growth.

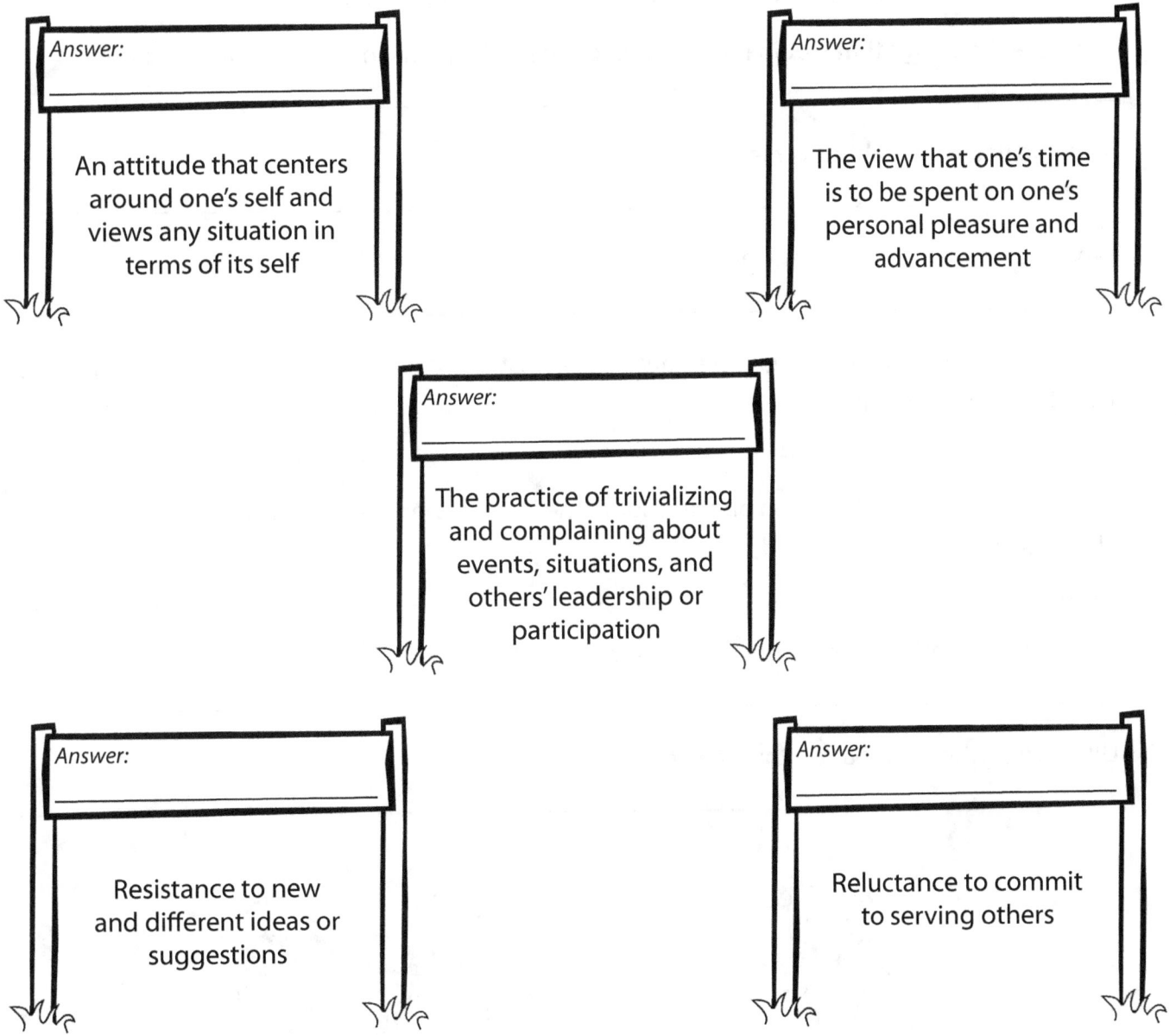

Answer: _____
An attitude that centers around one's self and views any situation in terms of its self

Answer: _____
The view that one's time is to be spent on one's personal pleasure and advancement

Answer: _____
The practice of trivializing and complaining about events, situations, and others' leadership or participation

Answer: _____
Resistance to new and different ideas or suggestions

Answer: _____
Reluctance to commit to serving others

REPRODUCIBLE 2

Humility Bible Study

Read Philippians 2:1–13.

What did Paul say in these verses that would make him happy?
_____

What are the things that would have motivated the Philippians to have such an attitude?
_____

What do you notice about verses 5–11?
_____

What is so incredible about the attitude of Christ as it's described here?
_____

What did Paul mean about everyone bowing to Christ and confessing him? Surely everyone in the world does not do that!
_____

What is the difference between obeying someone in his or her presence and doing so in his or her absence?
_____

What does it mean to "work out your salvation" (v 12)?
_____

Ultimately, who brings about our salvation?
_____

Portable Sanctuary

Day 1

If . . . Then Statements

There is a computer programming concept called an "If…then" statement. By utilizing such a statement, a computer takes a certain action based on whether or not something is true. We all utilize "If…then"-type decisions every day. *If I miss the bus, then I'll ask my dad to take me to school. If I don't study, then I'll fail the algebra test. If I act like a jerk to my boyfriend, then he'll be mad at me.* What happens on the "if" side determines what will happen on the "then" side.

Questions and Suggestions

- Read Philippians 2:1–2. Did Paul really doubt that his friends would do what he expected? How can you tell?
- Did you know that you can make your youth leader's joy complete by having the mind and the humility of Christ? Pray about it.

Day 2

You're So Vain!

In the 1970s, a musical artist named Carly Simon wrote and recorded a song about a guy who was incredibly conceited. When he walked into the room, he expected everyone to look at him—and he was glad when they did. He had a lot of money, and he loved to throw it around. He was apparently in a relationship with the singer at one time, but in his selfishness he threw it away. The song doesn't name a name, and people have speculated for years just whom it might be talking about.

NOTES

Questions and Suggestions

- Read Philippians 2:3–4. What did Paul say should be the priority of our own interests?
- Pray that God will help you make room in your life for the interests of others.

Day 3
From the Top to the Bottom

The history of the sports world and the music scene are littered with instances of people who were at the top—and quickly fell out of the spotlight. Athletes are practically worshipped by their fans, until they are caught cheating or are involved in scandals that cause them to lose their sponsorships and their position on the team. Musicians are riding high when they have a song high on the charts, but when they fail to come up with a follow-up hit, people quickly forget who they are.

Questions and Suggestions

- Read Philippians 2:5–8. How did Christ come to his humble position? How is this different than the sports stars and music icons of today?
- Thank God that you have eternal life as a result of the humility of Christ.

Day 4
From the Bottom to the Top

Have you seen the movie *Slumdog Millionaire*? A young boy in India is orphaned and spends his childhood living on the streets. He and his brother live as they can, sleeping in a dump for a while and stealing from tourists in order to survive. It seems that this boy can never get a break. Then he gets a shot at a trivia-type game show, and the experiences of his life have provided all the answers he needs. In the end he wins the grand cash prize—and finally gets the girl he has always loved.

Questions and Suggestions

- Read Philippians 2:9–11. What do you think it will feel like for someone who has denied Christ in this life to realize the truth about Christ after he or she dies?
- Thank God for the great treasure that is yours because you have gladly chosen Christ *now*.

Day 5
Always Obeying

There's an old saying, "If only I were a fly on the wall.…" In other words, *I wish I could secretly be in the room and hear what those people are talking about*. Are they talking bad about *me*? Some people say one thing to our faces—and something entirely different when we are not around! But there are other people we would trust with our very lives. We have no doubt that they are true. They are not one way when we are around and another way when they are away from us.

Questions and Suggestions

- Read Philippians 2:12–13. Why would Paul's friends be even *more* motivated to do the right thing when Paul *wasn't around*?
- God is always watching. He's always with you. But would you still do the right thing even if he *weren't*? Pray about it.

Leading into the Session

Warm Up

Option 1 Reproduce a drawing.
LITTLE PREP *Reproducible 1, pens or pencils*
Option 2 Build the perfect person.
MORE PREP *One or more Mr. Potato Head sets*

Starting Line

Option 1 Play a sit-down game.
YOUNGER YOUTH
Option 2 Discuss times of rejection.
OLDER YOUTH

Leading through the Session

Straight Away

Explore the Bible passage.
Bibles

The Turn

Dramatize Philippians 3:1–16.
Props to symbolize the application of the passage

Leading beyond the Session

Home Stretch

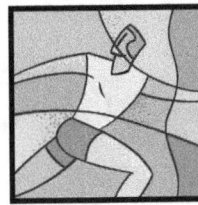

Option 1 Match biblical characters with descriptions of their lives.
YOUNGER YOUTH *Reproducible 2, pens or pencils*
Option 2 Listen to a senior adult encourage the group to persevere.
OLDER YOUTH *Senior adult to visit the class*

Finish Line

Option 1 Identify ways to grow as disciples.
LITTLE PREP *Bibles, paper, pens or pencils*
Option 2 Conduct a real race.
MORE PREP *Outdoor area in which to race, prizes*

SESSION 3

LOOKING TO THE FUTURE

Bible Passage
Philippians 3:1–16

Key Verses
Forgetting what is behind and straining toward what is ahead, I press on toward the goal to win the prize for which God has called me heavenward in Christ Jesus.
—Philippians 3:13–14

Main Thought
God calls us to adjust our attitude from surrender to perseverance.

Bible Background

In the first years of missionary expansion in the New Testament church, Christianity as a religion was still in the process of formation. Its only Scripture was the Greek translation of the Old Testament—the so-called *Septuagint*. At the time that Paul wrote the Philippian letter, most of the New Testament books had yet to be written. Without the New Testament texts to guide them, people read the Old Testament with widely varying interpretations when it came to the life, death, and resurrection of Jesus and what that implied for Christ's followers. (As we know from later church history, Christians have come to different conclusions about some of these matters even *with* the New Testament.)

Today's Bible lesson illustrates three different views of the consequences of Jesus' life for his followers. One of these of course is the Pauline view, which eventually framed orthodox Christian teaching. On either side of Paul stood two other interpretations, which in the church's early days threatened to become normative.

On one side were those who saw Jesus as an extension of Judaism. We might think of them as conservatives in their determination to enforce the Old Testament law on all members of the church. They insisted on circumcision for all new Christians, for example. In contrast to these *Judaizers*, Paul taught that God's righteousness comes through faith in Christ—"the righteousness that comes from God and is by faith" (3:9).

Challenging Paul from the other side were those who believed that Christ granted them radical freedom. These liberals—really, libertines—denied that the law had any validity and lived utterly undisciplined—sometimes unethical, immoral—lives. They were people who thought that God's salvation in Christ was entirely spiritual and thus made the concept and practices of ethical living obsolete.

In criticizing the libertines Paul said, "Our citizenship is in heaven" (3:20). This is more than a reminder of the Christian's ultimate destiny. Heavenly citizenship begins here and now in the confession that Christ is Savior and Lord. To become a citizen of heaven is to display in everyday life the virtues of the heavenly city. Heavenly citizenship implied that a new set of Christian virtues must replace the old Roman ones. Wealth, arrogance, militarism, and power understood as force had to give way to love, joy, peace, long-suffering, self-control, and the other virtues that Paul called the harvest of the Spirit's activity in the soul. Heavenly citizenship meant having the same mind as Christ about obedient, faithful living.

Leading into the Session

Option 1 (Little Prep)
Reproduce a drawing.

Distribute copies of "Perseverance Challenge" (Reproducible 1) and ask your group to try reproducing the drawing without tracing or erasing. Give them a few minutes to try. The figure is a challenging one to draw. As they work toward this goal, frequently use the term *persevere* to encourage them not to give up. After a few minutes, compare the results.

Say, **Sometimes in life we face challenges and obstacles that keep us from reaching our goals.**

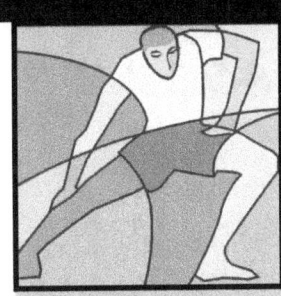

WARM UP

Option 2 (More Prep)
Build the perfect person.

Bring to class one or more Mr. Potato Head sets. Divide the students into groups according to how many sets you have. Challenge the members of each group to assemble the Mr. Potato Head pieces in order to construct what they would consider to be the perfect person. After the groups have done this, take time to compare and discuss the results. Why did they choose as they did? What sorts of things do people consider as being characteristics of the "perfect" person? Ask, **What would be the characteristics of the "perfect" Christian or spiritual person?** Students may suggest someone who constantly prays, reads the Bible, goes to church, and helps others.

Say, **Sometimes we feel challenged or compelled to be perfect or to present a perfect image to others.**

Note:
If you sent the Portable Sanctuary home with students last week, take some time at the beginning of this session to review and discuss their experience.

Option 1 (Younger Youth)
Play a sit-down game.

Ask the entire group to stand. Say, **I want you to sit down and remain seated whenever a statement I read applies to you.** The students should be as honest as possible. Here are some statements you can use, but feel free to create your own:

Sit down if you…
- have ever worn the same socks for two days.
- sing in the shower.
- have eaten snails.
- have missed your bus or train stop.
- use spray deodorant.
- have been sick while away from home.
- have ordered in a restaurant without enough money to pay for it.
- have locked yourself out of a car, house, or room.

STARTING LINE

If most teens are still standing, read a general characteristic that will apply to all of them (such as, "Sit down if you are under twenty years old"). After everyone is sitting, point out that sometimes, whether we like it or not, we are left out of a group—rejected by our friends, cut from an athletic team, or even just excluded for no apparent reason.

When you are ready to move on, say, **Let's read what the Apostle Paul said about "fitting in" and whom we should identify with.**

• •

Option 2 (Older Youth)
Discuss times of rejection.

Ask your students to share with the group about times they have been rejected. Encourage them to think about a variety of situations—rejection by friends, being cut from a sports team, being fired from a job, and so forth. Say, **Looking back on it now, does the rejection still hurt? Why do you think you were rejected? What (if anything) would you do differently if you could go back to that situation and do it over again?** Invite the students to respond. You can probably help to get them talking by sharing a story from your own life. Point out that we have all been rejected at some point. Sometimes there were valid reasons, and sometimes the reasons were not so good.

When you are ready to move on, say, **Let's read what the Apostle Paul said about "fitting in" and whom we should identify with.**

Leading through the Session

Straight Away

Explore the Bible passage.

Read together Philippians 3:1–16 and discuss the following questions:
- **Why would Paul write the same message to his friends again?** Important things are often worth repeating! Paul knew that helping his friends understand this truth would "safeguard" them—that is, it would protect their relationship with the Lord.
- **What did Paul mean by "mutilators of the flesh" (v 2)? Were there some people who practiced torture?** No; Paul was referring to circumcision, an act originally given to the Jewish people by God to signify their designation as God's people. Some people felt that being circumcised made a man right with God, but Paul said that it is through Christ and in the Spirit of God that we become God's people.
- **What was Paul's record as a "traditional Jew"—someone who met all the historical requirements of following God?** Paul had a spotless record. He was born into the Israelite nation, circumcised as God had directed, a member of the Pharisees (a devout religious group), a persecutor of Christians (whom traditional Jews considered blasphemous and insulting to God), and one who kept the laws of God perfectly. If anyone had reason to brag, Paul did.

- **Even though Paul had been raised and lived this way, what was his "new attitude" about it?** He considered it worthless now. The things he used to count on—family name, prestige and prosperity, knowledge and education, accomplishments, and religious ties—were worth nothing compared to knowing and serving Christ.
- **What kind of a life do you think Paul gave up in order to serve Christ?** As a devoted and well-trained Jew, Paul would have been an authority figure popular among his people and well-respected. He had everything someone could ask for to live what would have been considered a successful life. But he gave it all up because of the greater value he found in serving the Lord.
- **How can a person know the power of Christ's resurrection? How can we share in his sufferings? How can we become like him in his death?** When we place our faith in Christ, then we too can look forward to resurrection and eternal life. A life lived for God is not necessarily easy; there are many things we give up as we follow God. We may not die on a cross, but we are called to die to ourselves and to this world and to live every day in pursuit of God's will.
- **How did Paul think about his own spiritual growth?** He described it as a process and admitted that he did not have everything figured out. This should be of great comfort and encouragement to all of us. As long as we live, we should never stop learning about God and growing in our relationship with him.
- **What does it mean to "live up to what we have already attained" (v 16)?** Even though we all have some more learning and growing to do, we already know some of the right things to do, so we should do them!

Say, **Paul encouraged his friends to commit themselves to perseverance in their relationship with Christ.**

The Turn

Dramatize Philippians 3:1–16.
Bring to class these props to symbolize the application of this passage to your students' lives: a wallet or purse with money; bandages or a first aid kit; a cup of water; and a backpack containing a trophy or award ribbon, car keys, a baseball cap, a magazine representing a teenager's life (fashion, sports, or hobby), and a bottle of sports drink.

Copy the following script for a volunteer, who should shoulder the full backpack and hold the wallet or purse. Ask this person to begin running around the room and to follow the italicized instructions as you read the passage aloud:
- **But whatever was to my profit I now consider loss for the sake of Christ.**—*Runner puts down wallet or purse and begins to slowly run in place.*
- **What is more, I consider everything a loss compared to the surpassing greatness of knowing Christ Jesus my Lord, for whose sake I have lost all things. I consider them rubbish, that I may gain Christ**—*Runner stops running, takes off backpack, and takes out contents.*
- **and be found in him, not having a righteousness of my own that comes from the law, but that which is through faith in Christ—the righteousness that comes from God and is by faith.**—*Runner places empty backpack over shoulder and begins to run in place in the opposite direction.*

- **I want to know Christ and the power of his resurrection and the fellowship of sharing in his sufferings, becoming like him in his death**—*Runner begins moving again, stops to place bandages or first aid kit in backpack, and then continues running.*
- **and so, somehow, to attain to the resurrection from the dead.**—*Runner continues running.*
- **Not that I have already obtained all this, or have already been made perfect, but I press on to take hold of that for which Christ Jesus took hold of me.**—*Runner gradually slows, looks tired, and takes backpack off shoulder.*
- **Brothers, I do not consider myself yet to have taken hold of it. But one thing I do: Forgetting what is behind and straining toward what is ahead**—*With a thirsty look, runner glances over shoulder at the things left behind.*
- **I press on toward the goal to win the prize for which God has called me heavenward in Christ Jesus.**—*Runner turns back around and slowly keeps going.*
- **All of us who are mature should take such a view of things. And if on some point you think differently, that too God will make clear to you. Only let us live up to what we have already attained.**—*Runner picks up speed and is given a cup of water.*

After your dramatic reading, ask, **Which part of this passage speaks the most to you? How can these things help you as you run the race of life and strive to grow in the Lord?** Invite the students to respond.

Say, **Paul's words should encourage each of us to commit ourselves to persevere in our relationship with Christ.**

Leading beyond the Session

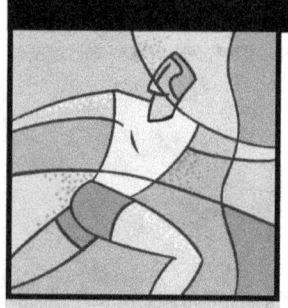

HOME STRETCH

Option 1 (Younger Youth)
Match biblical characters with descriptions of their lives.

Distribute copies of "Disciple Matchup" (Reproducible 2) or show it as a projection. Instruct the students to match the biblical characters, all followers of Jesus, in the left column with the appropriate actions or events from their lives. After the students have been given time to make the matches, ask volunteers to share their responses. As a group, discuss the commitment of these individuals—in simple ways and more complex ways—to serving Christ. Correct answers are as follows:

- **Peter**—"The rock"; one of Twelve who became a fiery preacher; miraculously delivered from prison; traditionally thought to have been crucified upside down.
- **Barnabas**—"The encourager"; sold land to contribute money to the church; traveled with Paul on missionary journeys.
- **Stephen**—"The martyr"; stood against temple authorities; preached famous sermon; Saul watched as he was stoned to death.
- **Philip**—Traveled as evangelist; witnessed to and baptized high-ranking Ethiopian official.
- **Phoebe**—Leader of church in Cenchrea and friend of Paul.

- **John Mark**—Young man who traveled with Paul and Barnabas when they confronted Bar-Jesus.
- **Saul**—Jewish legalist who persecuted early Christians; temporarily blinded during conversion on Damascus road; led the effort to spread the gospel into Asia Minor and Europe; more commonly known as Paul.
- **Priscilla and Aquila**—Couple who traveled with and protected Paul; served as mentors to Apollos.
- **John the Baptist**—Prophet who preached the coming of Christ; he was beheaded at the request of Herodias's daughter.
- **James**—One of the "Sons of Thunder"; son of Zebedee; was executed by Herod.

When you are ready to move on, say, **As disciples we need to take a good, hard look at our commitment to Jesus Christ. God holds us responsible for obedience, not for success. He will judge us for our efforts, not our accomplishments.**

Option 2 (Older Youth)
Listen to a senior adult encourage the group to persevere.

Invite a senior adult from your congregation to visit the class and to share about what has kept him or her from giving up and helped him or her to persevere as a Christian. Utilize any or all of the following questions, and feel free to add others:

- **When did you become a Christian?**
- **How has life been different since you have been a Christian?**
- **What or who has influenced your growth as a disciple of Jesus Christ? How did this happen?**
- **When have you been tempted to give up? How did you respond? How did God provide stability during these times?**
- **What miracles have you experienced or witnessed during your lifetime?**
- **What advice could you give to a young Christian who is discouraged?**

When you are ready to move on, say, **Here's a current example of someone who has managed to persevere in the faith and serve Christ effectively.**

Note:
Be sure to thank your guest and to pray for him or her.

Option 1 (Little Prep)
Identify ways to grow as disciples.

Direct the students' attention back to Philippians 3:1–16. Distribute paper and pens or pencils and say, **Paul gave up a lot in order to follow Christ. What things might you need to give up in order to grow as a disciple? In what areas should you "press on" and not give up?** Give the students time to write down their responses. Invite those who are willing to share their ideas with the rest of the group.

Close the session in prayer. Remember any special needs, and ask God to give your students the strength and perseverance to serve Christ until the very end.

FINISH LINE

> *Note:*
> Don't forget to distribute copies of the Portable Sanctuary to students before they leave.

Option 2 (More Prep)
Conduct a real race.

Find an outdoor area in which you can conduct a race with your students. Be sure to furnish some sweet prizes for the winners. You can make the race as conventional or as unusual as you wish. The goal is to send your students home with a way to remember our call to perseverance in our faith.

Close the session in prayer. Remember any special needs, and ask God to give your students the strength and perseverance to serve Christ until the very end.

REPRODUCIBLE 1

Perseverance Challenge

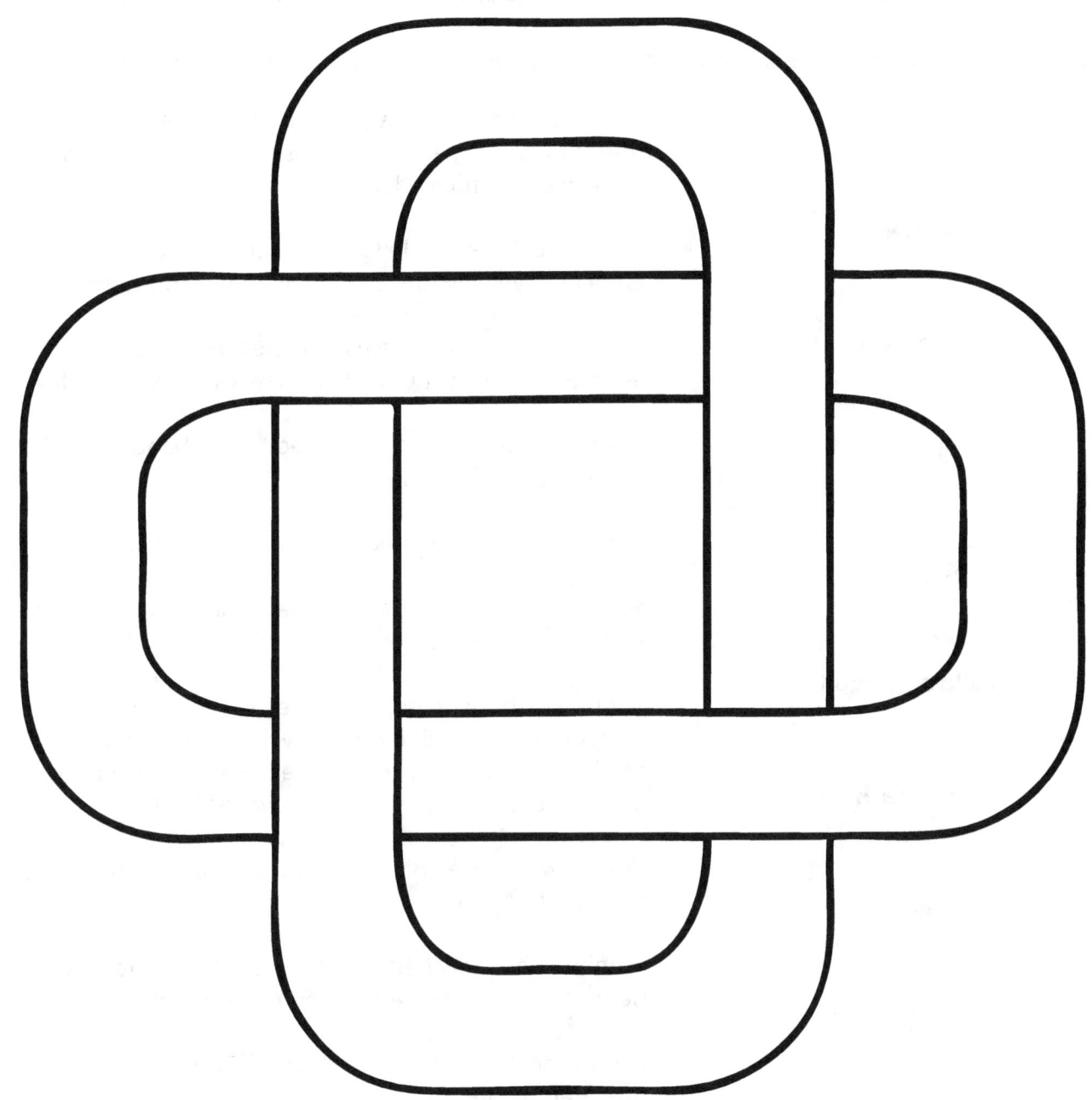

Disciple Matchup

Match the biblical characters on the left with the appropriate actions or events from their lives.

Saul

"The rock"; one of Twelve who became a fiery preacher; miraculously delivered from prison; traditionally thought to have been crucified upside down.

James

"The encourager"; sold land to contribute money to the church; traveled with Paul on missionary journeys.

Barnabas

"The martyr"; stood against temple authorities; preached famous sermon; Saul watched as he was stoned to death.

Peter

Traveled as evangelist; witnessed to and baptized high-ranking Ethiopian official.

Stephen

Leader of church in Cenchrea and friend of Paul.

Young man who traveled with Paul and Barnabas when they confronted Bar-Jesus.

Priscilla and Aquila

Jewish legalist who persecuted early Christians; temporarily blinded during conversion on Damascus road; led the effort to spread the gospel into Asia Minor and Europe; more commonly known as Paul.

John Mark

Couple who traveled with and protected Paul; served as mentors to Apollos.

Phoebe

Prophet who preached the coming of Christ; he was beheaded at the request of Herodias's daughter.

Philip

One of the "Sons of Thunder"; son of Zebedee; was executed by Herod.

John the Baptist

Portable Sanctuary

Day 1
Just a Reminder......

Do you do any regular chores at home? Our daughter has the responsibility to scrape the cat box each day. Not a really pleasant task, but that's her daily chore. She has done this for over a year now, and she rarely has to be reminded anymore. We used to have our kids' chores written out on a note that was posted on the refrigerator. Now they no longer need such a list. They know what they are expected to do, and they always remember to do it. As parents, we appreciate this—and so does the cat!

Questions and Suggestions

- Read Philippians 3:1. How did Paul feel about "reminding" his friends about the things he was going to write? Why do you think he felt this way?
- Commit yourself to regularly studying the Word of God, even those parts you have already studied. The reminder is good for you!

Day 2
The Best of the Best

He had grown up as a privileged child, and now his own wife and children enjoyed the best of everything: fancy cars, fine food, expensive vacations, and popularity. He was a good husband and father, and he enjoyed providing his family with these things. But then everything changed. His only son was diagnosed with leukemia. Treatments were begun, but the prognosis was no longer good. Suddenly, the things that were important before no longer mattered. The man's focus changed to telling his son how much he loved him and spending every moment he could with him.

NOTES

Questions and Suggestions

- Read Philippians 3:2–6. Paul seemed to have a good life. What happened that would cause him to leave this all behind? (Hint: See Acts 9:1–19.)
- Pray that God will help you maintain perspective about what is truly important in life.

Day 3
A Different Kind of Righteousness

There was a time when some Christians looked around and noticed that God's people didn't live very godly lives. They thought, "When we love God, it should make a difference in the way we live!" These people committed themselves to living without any sin. Sometimes they made specific lists (written and unwritten) about the things that God's people should or shouldn't do. And sometimes they lost focus of the fact that God makes us righteous and holy—not our own efforts, and not adherence to any list.

Questions and Suggestions

- Read Philippians 3:7–11. What was the source of Paul's righteousness? How important was this source to him?
- Pray that God will help you more fully know the power of Christ's resurrection and the fellowship of sharing in his sufferings.

Day 4
Don't Give Up!

Even people who seem to be perfect—aren't. Everyone has struggles and challenges. You may be surprised to find out the weaknesses and faults that your favorite music stars or sports heroes live with. They tend to be very careful at keeping those things a secret, but the truth is revealed eventually. Does this make these people any less talented? No. It just shows that they are human as the rest of us are. They don't have it all figured out all of the time. Sometimes they fall, just as we do.

Questions and Suggestions

- Read Philippians 3:12–14. How would these words have been a tremendous encouragement to Paul's friends?
- Pray that God will keep the heavenly prize constantly in front of you, so that you can keep moving ahead.

Day 5
Time to Grow Up

Do you know any adults who seem to have never grown up? It's not just that they still enjoy having fun; it's that they never learned to take any responsibility for themselves. They fail to keep a job, to care for their aging parents, and to help anyone else at all, really. It's not that they have mental issues or suffer from some kind of addiction. It's just that they have never really grown up. God calls us to live up to the things we know are right. This is a part of growing up.

Questions and Suggestions

- Read Philippians 3:15–16. When have you been uncertain of something, but then God made it clear to you?
- Pray that God will help you to live up to the truth of God that you already know.

Leading into the Session

Warm Up

Option 1 — Discuss a song.
LITTLE PREP

Option 2 — Sing happy songs in a new way.
MORE PREP
Large sheet, lipstick, small paper cutouts of eyes and a body, tape

Starting Line

Option 1 — Play a pressure game.
YOUNGER YOUTH
Child's game with different shapes and openings, confetti (shredded paper)

Option 2 — Identify some pictures.
OLDER YOUTH
Reproducible 1 or prepared pictures of famous smiles

Leading through the Session

Straight Away

Explore the Bible passage.
Bibles

The Turn

Find verses that describe happiness.
Bibles, concordances

Leading beyond the Session

Home Stretch

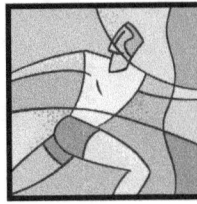

Option 1 — Analyze advertisements that sell happiness.
YOUNGER YOUTH
Magazines with lots of ads

Option 2 — Determine what it takes to be happy.
OLDER YOUTH
Reproducible 2, pens or pencils

Finish Line

Option 1 — Make a list to resist panic.
LITTLE PREP
Chalkboard or dry erase board

Option 2 — Show your concern.
MORE PREP
Opportunity to minister to someone in the church

SESSION 4

PRAISING GOD AND GETTING ALONG

Bible Passage
Philippians 4:2–13

Key Verse
Rejoice in the Lord always. I will say it again: Rejoice!
— Philippians 4:4

Main Thought
God calls us to adjust our attitude from worry to joy.

141

Bible Background

Paul wrote to the Philippian church while imprisoned, awaiting a trial and a possible death sentence. While he was fully aware of the possibility of execution, Paul wrote with joy and out of concern for the needs of the Philippians. He focused his mind and heart not on his own situation but on Christ and the church.

From Paul's vantage point a healthy church was of paramount concern. In sick churches leaders allowed disagreements to fester into open disputes. As today's passage indicates, apparently two Philippian leaders, Euodia and Syntyche, had argued over some point now unknown to us. We know that they were leaders because Paul said they had "contended at my side in the cause of the gospel" and also referred to them as "fellow workers" (4:3). Note that these church leaders were women. Paul's written statements about the role and place of women in the church should be placed alongside his references to practice. Paul's practice was to treat men and women equally as candidates for gospel service, as this and other references repeatedly demonstrate. For Paul, the unity of the church needed to be practiced, not just talked about. So he urged the two leaders to resolve their disagreement.

Paul also had in view the practice of Christian virtues at Philippi. To rejoice in everything and to be anxious for nothing are virtues of Christian living made possible by remembering that the Lord is near. *Near* may have meant that the Lord was always present or that Paul expected Christ's imminent return. In either case, Christian awareness that the Lord is near increases joy and lessens anxiety. Paul also exhorted his readers to put into practice the other virtues they had been taught or had read about or had seen embodied in Paul's life. Clearly Paul thought that the gospel embraced more than a set of beliefs. As crucial as faith was to the gospel, new life was also *a way of life* for Paul.

As Paul drew his letter to a conclusion, he thanked the Philippians for their abiding thoughtfulness and generosity. They had gone above and beyond the call of duty, contributing materially to Paul's support and sharing in his troubles. The fine Christians of Philippi had supported Paul from the early days of his second missionary journey at Thessalonica down to his imprisonment. To them Paul expressed his deep gratitude and his assurance that the God they served would never fail.

Leading into the Session

Option 1 (Little Prep)
Discuss a song.

Once the students have arrived, ask them to gather in a circle facing one another. Say, **Does anyone know the old song "If You're Happy and You Know It"? Let's sing a few verses!** Begin by leading the group in the first verse of the song: "If you're happy and you know it, clap your hands…." You may just get eyes rolled at you, but if the students are willing to sing, feel free to do more than one verse (stomp your feet, laugh out loud, jump around, or whatever else you might come up with). After your singing (or *attempted* singing) is done, ask, **What is the usual context of that song?** It is often done in children's Sunday school classes.

Say, **The truth of this song is simple but true—if you are happy, then your face will surely show it!**

WARM UP

Option 2 (More Prep)
Sing happy songs in a new way.

Bring to class a large sheet, lipstick, small paper cutouts of eyes and a body, and tape. Invite a volunteer to put on some lipstick and to lie on the floor on his or her back. Tape the cutout eyes on this person's chin and the cutout body on the person's nose, facing away from the mouth. Use the sheet to cover the person entirely, so that only the mouth and the paper cutouts are visible. This person should then sing part of a happy song of his or her choosing. (The person's mouth will look huge compared to the cutouts, and the sight of it singing upside-down is hilarious.) You can also allow a few more volunteers to try this as time permits.

Say, **Singing is one way that people sometimes show they are happy.**

Note:
If you sent the Portable Sanctuary home with students last week, take some time at the beginning of this session to review and discuss their experience.

Option 1 (Younger Youth)
Play a pressure game.

Bring to class a child's game in which pieces of different shapes must be placed into similarly shaped openings. Ask for a volunteer to dump the pieces onto his or her lap. At your signal, this person should slowly and carefully put all of the pieces through the correct openings while you record the time. Select another volunteer to repeat the process in a shorter amount time. Select a third volunteer to beat that time, only this time hold a container of confetti over his or her head. Warn that you will pour the confetti if he or she doesn't finish in record time. If this person is successful, continue with other volunteers until someone fails and you pour the confetti. After the game, discuss how the pressure and the anxiety mounted as the time was lowered.

When you are ready to move on, say, **Pressure can cause us to feel anxious. Let's see what the Apostle Paul said about dealing with times of anxiety.**

STARTING LINE

Option 2 (Older Youth)
Identify some pictures.

Distribute copies of "Famous Smilers" (Reproducible 1) or show it as a projection and see if the students can correctly identify who is represented by each smile. The correct answers (in order) are Barack Obama, Elvis Presley, Mona Lisa, and Marilyn Monroe, but you can accept other reasonable suggestions. You could also cut out from magazines just the smiles of some famous people and see if the students can correctly identify them. Afterwards, ask, **What is it that makes a smile so distinctive?** Our smiles are each very unique; because they are so specifically expressive, they can often be used as a means of identification. Behind every person's smile is a heart that experiences a whole range of emotions, including fear and worry. The eyes function in much the same way.

When you are ready to move on, say, **Let's see what the Apostle Paul said about dealing with times of fear or worry.**

Leading through the Session

Straight Away

Explore the Bible passage.

Read together Philippians 4:2–13 and discuss the following questions:
- **What was the situation with Euodia and Syntyche that Paul was addressing here?** We are not sure, but it was clear that they were in conflict over something. Paul pleaded that they get along for the sake of Christ, and he asked the reader of his letter to help in their reconciliation.
- **What does this say about one of our responsibilities as members of the body of Christ?** We too should help to mediate peace amongour fellow Christians. This is not always easy or comfortable. Sometimes others do not welcome our help, and they turn and attack us.
- **What specific encouragement did Paul give his friends in verses 4–6?** He told them to rejoice in God, to be gentle with others, and to ease any anxiety by praying to God. Emphasize that these things are valid for Christians today to live by; we should rejoice in God, be gentle, and turn our anxieties over to the Lord.
- **How is the Lord "near" to us?** When we give our hearts and lives to Christ, then Christ lives in us: He promised never to leave us or forsake us (see Hebrews 13:5). There is also some allusion to the fact that Christ promised to return someday.
- **What is a peace that "transcends all understanding" (v 7)?** Sometimes situations are so bad that it would seem natural for us to be totally upset, and yet we feel this unexplainable peace. This is the work of God. We can't explain why we are at peace when, by all logical explanations, we shouldn't be. This is one of the great blessings we have in our relationship with God.
- **What difference does it make what kinds of things we dwell on or think about?** Your students have probably heard the saying "Garbage in, garbage out." The things we focus our minds and thoughts on tend to find their way into our hearts and eventually our words and actions. If we focus on true, noble, right, pure, lovely, admirable, excellent, and praiseworthy things,

then our whole attitude will change. This is a part of the miraculous peace that we can experience in Christ.

- **Why do you think Paul's friends had not had the opportunity to show their concern for him?** There was no telephone service or e-mail in those days. Letters could be sent, but even that was much more complicated than scribbling a note with pencil and paper and dropping it in the mail. Paul was not there with the Philippians, so there literally was no good way for them to communicate with him.
- **How was it that Paul learned to be content no matter what the circumstances?** He had learned to operate in the strength of Christ and not in his own power. Remind your students that Paul truly did know what it was like to live a privileged life. To him, the contentment was in serving God, so it didn't matter what his circumstances were.

Say, **Paul encouraged his friends to move from an attitude of worry to one of joy.**

The Turn

Find verses that describe happiness.
Provide the students with Bibles and concordances and allow them time to look up verses and passages associated with happiness. Suggested terms to use include *happy, happiness, joy, gladness, contentment,* and *delight*. As the students find these references, ask for volunteers to read them aloud. For each one, discuss what we can learn about the way to true happiness. (Hint: Be sure to include some proverbs in your discussion.)

Say, **God doesn't want us to live in stress and worry; God wants us to experience true joy and happiness.**

Leading beyond the Session

Option 1 (Younger Youth)
Analyze advertisements that sell happiness.
Bring to class some magazines with lots of advertisements, including sports, fashion, home, travel, and celebrity magazines. Give the students two or three minutes to find and share with the group some ads that try to sell happiness. After you have looked at several ads, ask, **What strategies do advertisers use to sell their products? How are these ads supposed to make us feel or affect us?** If the person using a product seems happy, then we are expected to assume that the product will also make us happy. Help the students to understand that these forms of happiness do not last. When we look for happiness outside ourselves in areas such as romance, drugs, applause, thrills, and so forth, we will be disappointed because they do not last. We need happiness that comes from the inside, something that cannot be taken away.

When you are ready to move on, say, **Only Christ abiding in our lives can bring true happiness and peace.**

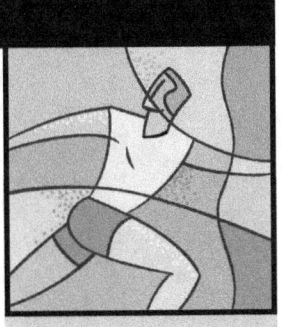

HOME STRETCH

Option 2 (Older Youth)
Determine what it takes to be happy.

Distribute copies of "Happiness Is…" (Reproducible 2), go over the instructions, and allow time for the students to complete the handout. After a few minutes, discuss their responses, focusing specifically on the questions at the bottom of the page. Point out that when we have the lasting peace and happiness of God through Christ, it tends to smooth out the emotional roller coaster of life. Instead of being dependent on our own feelings (which are constantly changing), we learn to stay focused on God and to live in his peace and power.

When you are ready to move on, say, **Only Christ abiding in our lives can bring true happiness and peace.**

Finish Line

Option 1 (Little Prep)
Make a list to resist panic.

Ask, **What things in life cause you (or used to cause you) to panic?** Invite the students to respond. For example, some students may have been afraid of ghosts when they were little, while others may have a current fear of flying. Ask, **What, really, is panic?** Panic is an overwhelming feeling of being in danger or out of control, in a bad or threatening situation where there is nothing you can do about it. Next invite the students to come up to the board, one at a time, and write down one thing they have done or would do to resist panic. These ideas should naturally focus on the panic situations that have just been expressed. Take some time to discuss these panic-resisting techniques.

As you prepare to wrap up the session, share the following concepts with the group:

- **We can resist panic by realizing that stress and unhappiness, like happiness, tend to be passing experiences.**
- **We can resist panic by focusing on the most unchangeable facts in life. God isn't intimidated by our unhappiness. If fact, God may be able to accomplish more in our lives during times of unhappiness than during times when we're simply wrapped up with feeling good.**
- **We can resist panic by helping someone who we know is unhappier than we are! We can probably even help ourselves in the process of helping this person.**
- **We can resist panic by making the joyful decision to keep going in spite of our feelings, presenting our unhappiness to God.**
- **We can resist panic by spending time with other Christians. They can support us during our unhappy times, and vice-versa.**

Close in prayer, asking God to move your students from an attitude of worry to one of joy.

Option 2 (More Prep)
Show your concern.

Paul knew that his friends were concerned for him, but they had not had the opportunity to express that concern. Give your students such an opportunity by taking them to minister to someone in your church. Perhaps there is an elderly shut-in who could use some company or a single mom who needs some cleanup work done in her yard. Get this person's permission to come, and make sure you have the proper permission to take your students off-site. Then, go as a group to minister in the name of Christ. Most situations will not require any expense, and they don't need to be complicated. The point is to show your concern in a tangible and helpful way.

Close the session in prayer, asking God to bless your work and the one to whom you will be ministering and to move your students from an attitude of worry to one of joy.

Note:
Don't forget to distribute copies of the Portable Sanctuary to students before they leave.

NOTES

REPRODUCIBLE 1

Famous Smilers

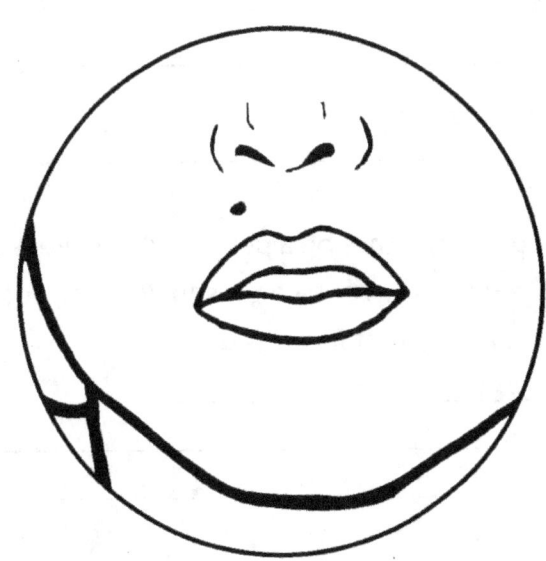

REPRODUCIBLE 2

Happiness Is ...

Common pursuit of happiness	What I need	A famous person who has it	What Paul had
Money			
Good Looks			
Power			
Achievements			
Pleasure/fun			

Describe the difference between joy and happiness.
_____
_____
_____

Read the statement: Happiness happens to you, but you choose joy. What do you think this means?
_____
_____
_____

Would you rather be a person whose life is completely at the mercy of whatever feelings you have right now, or be a person who can set feelings aside and keep going, doing what's right, recognizing that feelings don't last?
_____
_____
_____

Portable Sanctuary

Day 1
Getting Along

Sometimes we expect that everything will be perfect in the church. After all, Christ is the head of the church, and if everyone in the church loves God and loves others, there should be no conflict, right? But the church is still made up of people, and people make mistakes. Sometimes pride or selfishness creeps in. Even though Jesus encouraged us to forgive someone seventy times seven (a memorable way to say, "Keep on forgiving!"), it is still hard for us to let something go when we just know that *we* were right and the other person *was* wrong.

Questions and Suggestions

- Read Philippians 4:2–3. Were these arguing women just some casual members of the church, or were they committed Christians? How can you tell?
- Pray that God will use you as a peacemaker when your brothers and sisters in Christ are in conflict.

Day 2
No Worries

One reason not to worry is when a certain situation is not really what it seems. If a young child is worried about monsters in the closet, the parents can help this child to see that there are really no monsters in there. Some situations are very real and very serious. But another reason not to worry is when there is someone with you to protect you or to help take care of things. That's the kind of peace we have with God. God does not remove us from every situation, but he is there to guide and protect, to bless and give peace.

NOTES

Questions and Suggestions

- Read Philippians 4:4–5. How can we make a practice of rejoicing in a situation where the threat is very real?
- Make it your habit to pray regularly to God—when things are good and when things are not so good.

Day 3
Can't Figure It Out!

Just because our faith is in God does not mean that we go out seeking trouble. No one wants to purposely be harmed or suffer pain. When you think about something bad that might happen, it may cause you to doubt that your faith would stand up. But God has a way of giving the strength and peace we need to face a situation just when and where we need it. It defies understanding, but when we find ourselves up against impossible odds, the peace of God kicks in, guarding our hearts and minds.

Questions and Suggestions

- Read Philippians 4:6–7. Are you a peaceful person, or do you worry over even the smallest things? Do you know anyone who seems to be at peace no matter what? What is the source of this person's peace?
- If you are anxious over anything today, take it to God. Be sure to include a good dose of thanksgiving in your prayer. Then keep your eyes open for the peace of God to show up.

Day 4
Thinking Positive Thoughts

I have never enjoyed flying. One time when we were on a plane returning home from Christmas vacation, we hit some severe turbulence. The plane was never in any real danger, but we bounced up and down pretty strongly for several minutes. Sitting next to my young son (who doesn't really like to fly either), we both closed our eyes and began to pray for the peace of God, focusing our minds on positive things. The women across the aisle from us prayed together out loud. The peace of God came, and the plane soon settled down.

Questions and Suggestions

- Read Philippians 4:8–9. Who has been a good example to you of how to live a godly life? How can you follow this person's example?
- In your prayer time today, take a few minutes to focus your thoughts on each of these things: *true ... noble ... right ... pure ... lovely ... admirable ... excellent ... praiseworthy*.

Day 5
Always Content

In our country, we are quite used to having the basics of life—plus a lot more. Even the poorest among us have much more than most people in many countries of the world. In Paul's day, most people did not work so that they could receive a paycheck twice a month. They worked so they could have food for that day. There was no cupboard, no refrigerator, no grocery store, no savings account. If you did not work, you did not eat. If you became sick or disabled, you could be in real trouble!

Questions and Suggestions

- Read Philippians 4:10–13. How does the church express its concern for those in need? How can you be a part of that process?
- Whatever the situation you find yourself in now, thank God for his presence and provision and for the strength he gives you.

Leading into the Session

Warm Up

Option 1 Discuss methods of imprisonment.
LITTLE PREP *Chalkboard or dry erase board; large chain (optional)*

Option 2 Rewind two years.
MORE PREP *Computer with Internet access (before or during class)*

Starting Line

Option 1 Read about an ancient death.
YOUNGER YOUTH *Reproducible 1*

Option 2 Write your own epitaphs.
OLDER YOUTH *Paper, pens or pencils*

Leading through the Session

Straight Away

Explore the Bible passage.
Bibles

The Turn

Discuss a mature faith.

Leading beyond the Session

Home Stretch

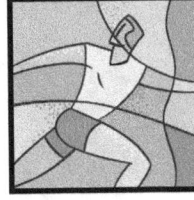

Option 1 Honor a long-standing teacher.
YOUNGER YOUTH *Individual from your congregation who has taught Sunday school the longest*

Option 2 Discuss faithfulness today.
OLDER YOUTH

Finish Line

Option 1 Discuss giving all for God.
LITTLE PREP *Reproducible 2*

Option 2 Observe responses to the gospel.
MORE PREP *Group visit to your church's worship service*

SESSION 5

USED TO THE END

Bible Passage
Acts 28:16–31

Key Verses
For two whole years Paul stayed there in his own rented house and welcomed all who came to see him. Boldly and without hindrance he preached the kingdom of God and taught about the Lord Jesus Christ.
—Acts 28:30–31

Main Thought
God calls us to remain faithful to him until the very end.

153

Bible Background

The Acts of the Apostles concludes with Paul in Rome, the imperial capital. He had arrived there under guard, having appealed to the emperor in a case that began with a riot against Paul in Jerusalem. Having survived murder plots, shipwreck, and the cool indifference of provincial bureaucrats, Paul witnessed to Christ in the greatest city of the Roman Empire.

According to Acts, Paul had not appealed to the emperor because he had been found guilty of a crime under Roman law. He had, in fact, been found innocent; the Romans were prepared to release him. But Jewish opposition was intensely hostile. Paul appealed to Caesar, at least in part, to save his own life.

The Romans did not maintain prisons for punishment, so "prison" was any place that could serve to hold people awaiting trial: a cave, a dungeon, a jail, or perhaps a military barracks. During his stay in Rome, Paul appears to have been under light custody. He was allowed to stay by himself in his own quarters while under the supervision of a lone guard.

Given the circumstances, it may seem odd that he invited Jewish leaders to meet with him at the place he was staying. A ruckus with Jewish opponents had endangered his life in the first place. Once in Rome he seems immediately to have placed his head back in the mouth of the beast that had threatened to behead him.

In another sense Paul's actions were completely in character with his approach to sharing the gospel of Jesus Christ. During his previous missionary travels, Paul had tended to begin by first preaching to the Jews in the area. In Rome, the Jews' reactions to Paul's message were mixed (Acts 28:24). Ultimately, it would seem, a tepid response by the Jews was once again followed by Paul's efforts to share the good news of Christ with Gentiles in the area.

The perseverance and unflagging commitment of Paul can be clearly seen in today's Bible Passage. Though he had endured abuse and threats of death at the hands of the Jews in other locations, he continued to share the gospel of Christ with the descendants of Abraham. Though facing trial and a possible death sentence, he energetically preached the kingdom of God for two years to *all* who would hear (vv 30–31). In whatever state he found himself, Paul never wavered from his primary commitment to share the hope of salvation that could be found in Jesus Christ.

Leading into the Session

Option 1 (Little Prep)
Discuss methods of imprisonment.

Ask your students to name every way they can think of that people are imprisoned or held captive today or have been in the past. Write their responses down as they are given. Some possibilities might include prisons, dungeons, islands, house arrest, ankle monitoring bracelets, tying someone up, being guarded, stocks, kidnapping, being threatened with a weapon, and even mind control. If possible, show to the class a length of large chain (such as might be used in towing or to tie down cargo). Ask, **How effective would a large chain be as a method of keeping someone imprisoned?** Unless the prisoner had a sharp hacksaw, a chain would be very difficult to escape from.

Say, **Human beings are continually working to create new and more effective ways to guard prisoners and keep them captive.**

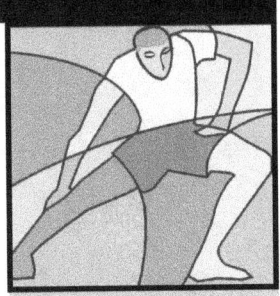

WARM UP

Note:
If you sent the Portable Sanctuary home with students last week, take some time at the beginning of this session to review and discuss their experience.

Option 2 (More Prep)
Rewind two years.

Encourage your students to "rewind their minds" back two years and try remember what was going on in their lives and in the world then. Ask, **What were you doing two years ago today? What kind of clothes did you wear? What was your hair like? Who were your friends? What was going on in your family and in your life?** Invite the students to respond. If you have access to a computer and Internet during class time, do a search for the date that was exactly two years ago from the current date. Explore the listed websites for other information from two years ago. If you can't use a computer during class time, do your research beforehand and print out the results to share with the group. If you wish, you can quiz them to see how much they remember about the date.

Say, **Depending on what's going on in our lives, two years can seem like a long time—or it can seem to go by in a flash.**

Option 1 (Younger Youth)
Read about an ancient death.

Distribute copies of "Staying at Their Post" (Reproducible 1) or show it as a projection and read this true story with your students. Afterwards, ask, **Why would anyone keep doing something they knew would kill them—even though they didn't have to?** Invite the students to respond. Point out that this was very different than soldiers or slaves who are under obligation or are forced to fight in dangerous situations. What these nuns did was completely voluntary. It was because of God—their love of and devotion to God—that they did it. Love is a strong motivator; in similar fashion, parents would willingly risk or give their own lives for the sake of their children.

When you are ready to move on, say, **Let's see how the Apostle Paul finished out his own days in service to God.**

STARTING LINE

Option 2 (Older Youth)
Write your own epitaphs.

Distribute paper and pens or pencils as you ask, **What is an epitaph?** An epitaph is the statement that is written on a tombstone about the deceased. Today most tombstones just give a name, date of birth, and date of death, but years ago a tombstone also carried a short message such as "Husband, father, grandfather" or "Served his country with honor." Invite the students to draw a large tombstone outline on their papers (square corners at the bottom and a rounded top) and to write down what they think their own epitaphs might say (or what they would *like* for them to say) some day. After a few minutes, invite those who are willing to share what they wrote.

When you are ready to move on, say, **Let's see some of the last words that were written about the Apostle Paul.**

Leading through the Session

Straight Away

Explore the Bible passage.

Read together Acts 28:16–31 and discuss the following questions:
- **Why was Paul in Rome?** He had been arrested for preaching the gospel and had appealed his conviction, so he was sent to Rome, the capital (see Acts 22–25). Historical records indicate that Paul never left Rome; he was finally executed there.
- **How was Paul imprisoned at this time?** He lived by himself in a rented house, with a soldier there to guard him. This was better than a prison cell, but it was still captivity. Verse 20 indicates that he was also chained up.
- **Why did Paul call the Jewish leaders together? Was it to plead his own case and try to win his freedom?** No; it was to preach to them in the hope that they might also come to believe in Christ. Acts 20:36–38 indicates that Paul knew he would die soon.
- **Why were the local leaders willing to listen to Paul?** Paul had strictly followed the Jewish law in his earlier days. He had since become a vocal and very effective follower of Christ. He would have been considered famous in a way. Some people may have been intrigued by and interested in his message, and others may have just been curious to meet him and hear him.
- **What was the content of Paul's message?** For the whole day initially and then for another two years, Paul preached that Christ was the fulfillment of Old Testament prophecy and the source of salvation. Paul also preached that some people would flat-out reject Christ.
- **How did the crowd respond to Paul's message?** They couldn't agree about it. Some people believed in what he said, but others refused to. Point out that people respond to the message of Christ in the same way today; some accept it and some do not.
- **What was Paul's constant mission while he was imprisoned in Rome?** He continually welcomed anyone who came to see him and boldly preached about Christ. We might have expected him to be fighting for his release or sulking about his condition, but instead he did what he could to share the message of Jesus Christ with anyone who would listen to him.

- **These are the last words written in the Bible about Paul. Why would the text not tell us the rest of the story of this famous and important New Testament figure?** It is possible that at the time Acts was written, Paul was still imprisoned in Rome; in other words, the rest of the story had not occurred yet.

Say, **God called Paul to remain faithful to him until the very end.**

The Turn

Discuss a mature faith.

Say, **Now I want you to fast-forward fifty or sixty years. Maybe you'll be married and have grandkids. But what might be happening in your spiritual life?** Invite the students to respond. Point out that people should mature spiritually just as they do physically and mentally. Encourage your students that your desire is to see them involved in the church in fifty or sixty years—not just sitting in a seat but teaching, singing, and leading as mature and ever-growing Christians. Say, **God will never leave us, but some people choose to leave God. I never want that to happen to you!** Point out that we must choose daily to maintain our commitment to Christ. A mature faith continues to grow and get stronger. It becomes more solid in Christ and is not as easily shaken by the storms and conflicts of this life.

Say, **God calls each of us to remain faithful to him until the very end.**

Leading beyond the Session

Option 1 (Younger Youth)
Honor a long-standing teacher.

Invite to your class the individual from your congregation who has taught Sunday school or a Bible study the longest. (Your pastor can help you to determine who this individual is.) Plan a short ceremony or prepare a small award to honor this person for his or her long-standing commitment to sharing the Word of God. Invite your guest to share with the students about his or her journey with the Lord over these years. Your students should also feel free to ask questions of your guest.

When you are ready to move on, say, **Here is a great example of someone who has maintained a long-term faithful commitment to serve Christ in our church.**

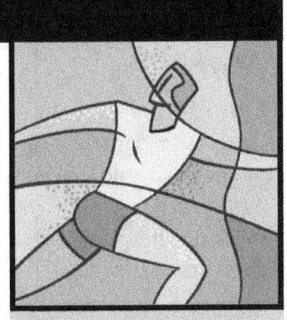

HOME STRETCH

. . . .

Option 2 (Older Youth)
Discuss faithfulness today.

Say, **Even if we're not imprisoned for our faith, how can we demonstrate a bold faithfulness to Christ as Paul did?** Invite the students to respond. Point out that it is not only missionaries or Christians under persecution who commit their lives to God's service. Wherever people live, in whatever circumstances of life, following God requires commitment. Jesus instructed his followers to keep his commandments; they begin with those he called the greatest—love God with all your heart and love your neighbor as yourself. When he was asked to define neighbor, Jesus told a parable that basically defined our neighbor as anyone we happen to meet. Say, **The person at the grocery store checkout, the greeter at Walmart, the persons who collect your trash—they are just as much your neighbor as the people who live next door. To treat them—and anybody**

Note:
Be sure to thank your guest and to pray for him or her.

157

else you happen to encounter—as you would like to be treated shows that Christian discipleship is your way of life.** Remind your students that Paul encouraged us to look out for the interests of others as well as our own interests (Philippians 2:4). This is not easy, for we are inclined to do just the opposite. That is why following Christ requires a solid commitment on our part.

When you are ready to move on, say, **Whether in prison or in the grocery store, it is our focus on others that shows our commitment to Christ.**

FINISH LINE

Option 1 (Little Prep)
Discuss giving all for God.

Distribute copies of "A Modern-Day Story of Faithfulness" (Reproducible 2) or show it as a projection and share this true story with your students. Say, **People today still live until the very end giving their lives in the passionate pursuit of Christ.** Again emphasize that whether God calls us to missions or preaching or to minister right where we work, he is looking for followers who will remain faithful to the end—whenever the end may be and however it may occur.

Close the session in prayer, thanking God for the faithfulness of your students and asking that in God's power and grace, they will still be faithful in a year, in ten years, in forty or fifty years, and until the end of their lives.

Note:
Don't forget to distribute copies of the Portable Sanctuary to students before they leave.

Option 2 (More Prep)
Observe responses to the gospel.

Point out again that not everyone was receptive to Paul's message about Christ. Paul was very consistent in what he preached, but not everyone was open to it or responded to it.

Give your group members the assignment during your church's next worship service to specifically observe the reactions of others in the congregation to the worship experience. (If your students usually sit together as a group in worship, it may be better for them to spread out for this assignment.) Emphasize that they are not to be disruptive or a distraction to worship and should seek to worship themselves, but that you want them to also be observant of how others react during the service. Afterwards, debrief the experience and discuss your students' observations. (It is better to do this shortly afterwards instead of waiting until next week's meeting.) Ask, **How did you see people reacting during the singing, the offering, the announcements, the special music, the sermon, and any other parts of the worship service?** Your students may have noticed that some people were more dynamic in their response while others were more reflective and composed. They may have even noticed some people sleeping, talking, or texting during the service. If an altar call was given, some people may have responded while others walked out the door. Emphasize that none of these behaviors are reasons for judgment—and it's not your place to judge, anyway. The point is, people respond in different ways to the message of Christ. Some are open, and some are not. Say, **God calls us to be faithful in delivering the message; the results are up to him.**

Close the session in prayer, thanking God for the faithfulness of your students and asking God to speak to hearts and change lives each week as your church meets for worship.

Staying at Their Post

A February 2009 news story reported the discovery of the cause of death of several nuns who died in seventeenth-century France. The women belonged to the Benedictine order of nuns of the Abbey of Sainte-Croix. The Mother Superior of the Abbey was known to be a very generous person who spent her life caring especially for the poor. Charlotte Flandrina was of noble birth, the fourth daughter of Prince William of Orange. When she became a nun, she sold most of her possessions to purchase food and medical care for the poor people of the region, many of whom had contracted the plague—the famous "Black Death"—from soldiers fighting in the Thirty Years' War.

Historical records indicate that the nuns who cared for plague victims also succumbed to the disease between 1628 and 1632. Researchers recently tested a group of skeletons found resting on a layer of the disinfectant lime and detected markers of the presence of the deadly bacteria that causes the plague. Members of the clergy and religious orders contracted the disease as they cared for their parishioners, just as their call to ministry and service required.

The great thirteenth-century theologian Thomas Aquinas used the example of such people as the nuns of the Sainte-Croix Abbey to make a point about the manner in which Christian love alters the virtue of courage. We are accustomed to think of soldiers and battlefields when we think about courage. But Aquinas pointed to those who willingly tend to plague victims as displaying another kind of courage. Almost certain to contract the disease borne by those for whom they cared, people who tended for plague victims exemplified courage reshaped by Christian love. This love kept the nuns of Sainte-Croix at their post, even though they knew they would probably die as a result.

A Modern-Day Story of Faithfulness

Northwest of Nairobi, Kenya, in a district of the Western province sits the village of Ingotse. There in the village stands Murray Memorial Church, named for missionaries James and Ruth Murray.

In 1921, James Murray went to British East Africa as a missionary. Not too long afterwards he met and began courting another missionary named Ruth Fisher. In 1925 they were married and moved to Ingotse, where they served in a boys' school and worked in village evangelism. During their years in Ingotse they encountered both joys and heartache. The missionary staff grew rapidly and developed schools and medical clinics. Conversions in the villages multiplied again and again. One young convert donated land for a new mission station in Mwhila. But three babies born to Ruth Murray died in infancy. Then, in 1936, Ruth contracted typhoid fever and also died. Four years later the body of James Murray was laid to rest in Kima cemetery next to his wife and children after he succumbed to a particularly virulent form of malaria called blackwater fever.

The Murrays had not pursued rewards or recognition, but the church in Kenya honored their service, their commitment to the gospel of Jesus Christ and his church, by naming the church building in Ingotse after Ruth and James.

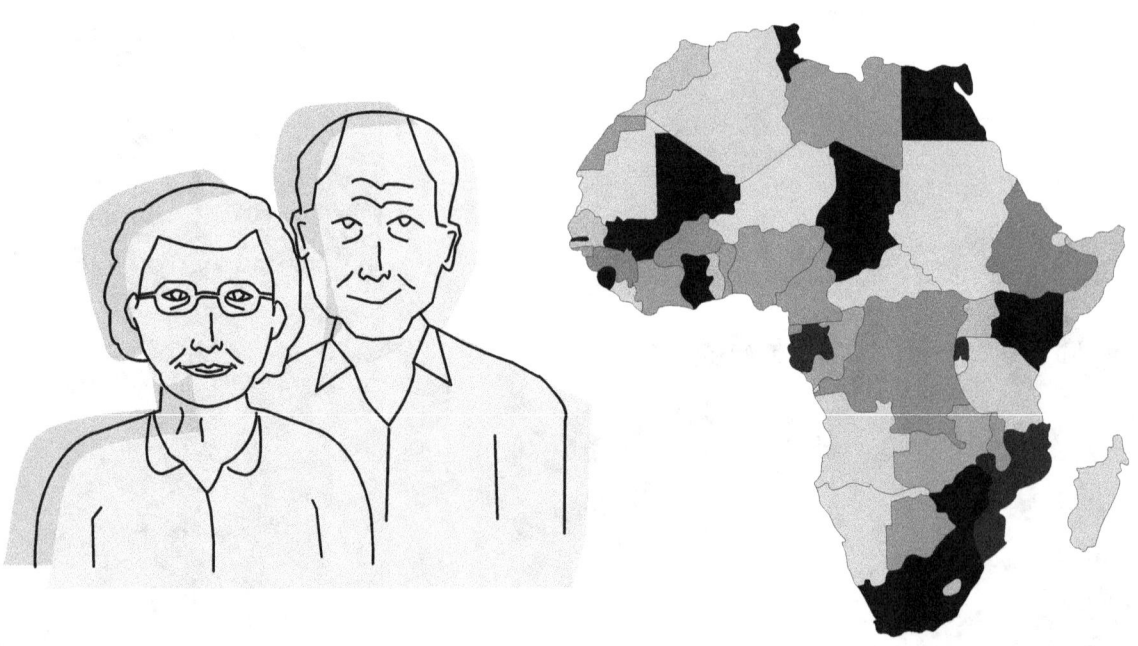

Portable Sanctuary

Day 1
House Arrest

In response to overcrowding in jails, authorities have developed a system called house arrest. A prisoner is allowed to go home, but he or she wears an electronic monitoring band on the ankle. If the prisoner tries to take the band off or leaves the house, the police are immediately notified, and that person is sent back to jail. These systems are sometimes set up so that the prisoner is also permitted to go to work. He or she is still confined, but not behind the bars of a literal prison building.

Questions and Suggestions

- Read Acts 28:16. Why do you think Paul was kept captive in this way? How would this have been to his benefit?
- Pray that God will place you in situations where you can be used to share God's love with others.

Day 2
Give Me a Chance!

Those who share the good news of Christ are sometimes nervous to speak in front of others. (Even your pastor may feel this way sometimes!) Why would people put themselves through such an experience? They do it because they love God and because God has called them to do so. They are willing to risk ridicule and rejection in order to be heard. They might use visual props, personal stories, videos, music, or other tools to help get the message across. They are willing to do what it takes to give people the chance to hear the message.

NOTES

Questions and Suggestions

- Read Acts 28:17-20. Why would Paul seek out the Jewish leaders to speak to?
- Thank God for the "people connections" he has already given you—relationships where you already have an open door to share Christ.

Day 3
Speak Up!

Have you ever met anyone famous? One day my father was at the local fitness club, doing his usual time on the treadmill. There was a big convention in town that day, and the governor was there to visit it. He had a little free time on his hands, and he decided to check out some sights around the city. The fitness club was a large, brand-new facility, so the governor and his staff came in for a quick visit. My father was on the first treadmill inside the door, so he got to meet the governor and shake his hand.

Questions and Suggestions

- Read Acts 28:21-22. Why would the Jewish leaders in Rome already know about Paul? What do you think they might have expected him to say?
- Are there any public figures or leaders whom you are not particularly fond of? Pray for discernment, but don't close your mind to everything they have to say; you might be able to learn something new or important.

Day 4
The Big Speech

The day was finally here, and she was sweating bullets. She knew the crowd, but she knew her material even better. She had prepared meticulous notes, but she really didn't need them. When she stepped out on the stage, the lights were blinding, but not so blinding that she could not see the overflow crowd—many more people than they had expected to show up. She said a silent prayer, took a deep breath, and began. When it was all over, she felt relieved, but she wondered: *Did they really hear what I was trying to say?*

Questions and Suggestions

- Read Acts 28:23-28. How do you think Paul felt before giving this important speech? How could the makeup of his audience have been a positive thing? How could it have been a negative thing?
- Remember, God calls you to deliver the message. God is responsible for the results. If you have delivered the message, then you have been successful—regardless of how the people respond.

Day 5
Wrapping It Up

Think back to a former pastor, youth leader, or Sunday school teacher who is no longer at your church, and who left on a positive note. Why did that person leave? Maybe it was because of retirement, a job transfer, or something else. How did that person conclude his or her time at your church? Was there a farewell service or party? Do you remember the last things that person said or did before he or she left? Someone who is going away is often given a chance to say some final words.

Questions and Suggestions

- Read Acts 28:30-31. If you didn't know that history suggests that Paul was later put to death at Rome, how might you imagine that the story would have ended? Are you satisfied with the ending in Acts? Why or why not?
- Whether or not you are ever called to be a pastor, pray that God will give you the boldness to preach the kingdom of God—wherever you go and whatever you do.

Leading a Teenager to Christ

Throughout the year, natural times may come up to share the plan of salvation with your students. When that opportunity arises, you will want to be ready with a simple explanation told in a noncoercive manner. You may want to write it out or go over in your mind ahead of time what you will say. Following is a suggested plan and some related scriptures to spark your own prayerful thinking.

Share these thoughts in your own words:

1. God loves you and offers a wonderful plan for your life (John 3:16 and John 10:10).
2. Each of us has sinned and been separated from God, preventing us from knowing and experiencing God's plan (Romans 3:23 and Romans 6:23).
3. Jesus Christ is God's provision for our sin and separation from God (Romans 5:8 and John 14:6).
4. When we place our faith in Jesus Christ as Savior and Lord, then we can know and experience God's love and plan for our lives (John 1:12 and Ephesians 2:8–9).

Receiving Christ involves turning to God from self (repentance) and trusting Christ to come into our lives to forgive our sins and to make us what God wants us to be. It is not enough to agree to a list of facts about Jesus Christ or to have an emotional experience. We receive Jesus Christ by *faith*, as an act of the *will*.

If a student indicates that he or she is ready to make a decision, ask that person if he or she has any questions. If all seems clear, encourage the student to pray a prayer of repentance, asking God's forgiveness. You might guide the student with the following prayer:

God, I know I've done wrong and gone my own way. I am sorry. I want to follow you. I know Jesus died for my sins. I accept Jesus as my Savior and Lord. Thank you for forgiving me. Thank you for the gift of eternal life.

After the student has prayed, thank God for hearing his or her prayer, and affirm the student as a new Christian.

Explain to your student that as we pray, read the Bible, worship with other Christians, and tell others about what God has done for us, God will help us know how to live. Christ's presence is with us to help us live God's way. One step that a new believer should take is to be baptized. Baptism tells others that we are serious about following Jesus. Jesus set the example in being baptized, and we are baptized to show that we are living for Jesus.

Talk to your pastor and your student's parents about his or her decision. Continue to encourage your student by giving him or her instruction and materials for setting up a daily devotional time. If possible, make arrangements with someone in the church to meet regularly with your student to act as a spiritual mentor.

There are a number of simple tract-type visuals to help you share Christ with your students:

- *It's Awesome!* (available at www.warnerpress.org or 1-800-741-7721)
- *Bridge to Life* (available at www.navpress.com)
- *The Answer* (available at www.studentdiscipleship.org)

NOTES

EVALUATION FORM

What Is a Christian?

Community size: : _____   Church size: _____   Class size: _____

Average preparation time: _____   Class length: _____

My class is made up of: _____ Sixth graders   _____ Ninth graders

　　　　　　　　　　 _____ Seventh graders   _____ Tenth graders

　　　　　　　　　　 _____ Eighth graders   _____ Eleventh graders

　　　　　　　　　　　　　　　　　　　　　　　　　　 _____ Twelfth graders

Please rate the following on a scale of *1* (never) to *10* (always):

- Were the instructions clear and user-friendly? _____
- Was the content challenging enough for students? _____
- Were the activities adequate for this age level? _____
- Did you use the Portable Sanctuaries? (Y/N) _____

Which sessions and areas worked best for you? _____
_____

Which sessions and areas should be changed or improved? _____
_____

Suggestions and Comments: _____
_____
_____
_____

Your full name: _____

Congregation Name, City, and State: _____

Phone number (_____) _____   E-mail _____

--fold here--

--fold here--

NAME_____

ADDRESS_____

CITY/STATE/ZIP_____

* Don't forget your return address! Postage is free!

BUSINESS REPLY MAIL
FIRST-CLASS MAIL PERMIT NO. 1233 ANDERSON IN

POSTAGE WILL BE PAID BY ADDRESSEE

KEVIN STIFFLER, EDITOR
WARNER PRESS
PO BOX 2499
ANDERSON, IN 46018

NO POSTAGE
NECESSARY
IF MAILED
IN THE
UNITED STATES

www.ingramcontent.com/pod-product-compliance
Lightning Source LLC
Chambersburg PA
CBHW081448070526
44586CB00019B/2271